There can be no progress without struggle.

Frederick Douglass

VALUE CHANGE
and

POWER CONFLICT

IN HIGHER EDUCATION

Edited by
W. John Minter
and
Patricia O. Snyder

Center for Research and Development in Higher Education,
University of California, Berkeley
and
Western Interstate Commission for Higher Education
P. O. Drawer "P", Boulder, Colorado 80302

October, 1969

Additional copies available. $3.50

PREFACE

The Western Interstate Commission for Higher Education and the Center for Research and Development in Higher Education, Berkeley, present here the papers of the Eleventh Annual College and University Self-Study Institute. Since 1960, the Commission has joined with the Center to co-sponsor institutes in a number of areas of interest to administrators in higher education.

The purpose of the institutes is to present significant research findings and informed opinion on broad and fundamental issues in higher education. The institutes are attended by college administrators, faculty members, research scholars, public officials and student leaders from throughout the West and the nation.

We gratefully acknowledge the contributions of the authors of these papers, of the Center and WICHE staff who planned and conducted this year's institute, and of WICHE's publications unit which provided the services necessary for publication of these papers.

Leland L. Medsker, Director
Center for Research and Development
in Higher Education, Berkeley

Robert H. Kroepsch, Executive Director
Western Interstate Commission for
Higher Education

October, 1969
Boulder, Colorado

INTRODUCTION

College and university campuses have become the scene of frequent conflict and confrontation. Last year, institutions of higher education across the country were rocked by a wave of student disruptions—sit-ins, strikes, and riots. As the new school term begins this fall, college administrators are bracing themselves for renewed disturbances.

When members of the staffs of WICHE and the Center for Research and Development in Higher Education met last year to open discussion of the 1969 institute, all agreed that there could be no more pertinent topic for consideration than conflict on the campus. It appeared to the staff that campus power conflicts were related to basic value changes taking place in the university and in the wider society. Thus, the institute theme *Value Change and Power Conflict in Higher Education* was selected.

What are the traditional and emerging value patterns which appear to be at the root of the power conflicts in higher education? What are the public's interests in these competing value patterns and power conflicts? What are the interests of faculty, students, minority group members, and administrators? What are the implications for the roles of these groups in academic governance? How can college administrators deal effectively with the competing aspirations and values of the various campus and public groups? These are the basic questions which were discussed at the institute and which are explored in the papers presented in this volume.

It was not the objective of the institute to urge particular courses of action designed to resolve campus power conflicts. It was rather to provide a forum for thoughtful discussion of questions and issues related to value change and power conflict in higher education. A clear understanding of the causes of conflict is a prerequisite to effective resolution of conflict. We sincerely hope the papers that follow will contribute to this understanding.

W. John Minter
Patricia O. Snyder
Editors

CONTENTS

VALUE CHANGE
and

IN HIGHER EDUCATION

Precis

If we are to understand conflict within a university, we must comprehend the peculiarities of structure and process that characterize the academic enterprise. These peculiarities compound the complexity of handling power conflicts within the university.

One reason why a university is so vulnerable to attack, so helpless when caught in the turmoil of strife, is simply that so few persons are prepared to defend the university as a whole, as an organized entity.

Another reason why a university is vulnerable to attack is the devotion of the enterprise to academic freedom. Because a university is devoted to academic freedom it protects and even encourages a wide range of points of view about academic subjects and about the academic enterprise. However, when the expression of conflicting points of view moves from the method of discussion to the method of confrontation, it may become destructive of the academic enterprise itself.

It seems to me that above all other reasons the most important single explanation why universities are in trouble today is the absence of a clearly defined, explicit, and accepted mission for the academic enterprise. If the objective of the university is uncertain and confused, is it any cause for wonder that the university is beset by conflicts?

Higher education in the United States today confronts students and faculty members who are criticizing present value patterns. The emphasis upon professional education as the primary objective of higher education is under attack. The ostensible commitment to humane learning is subject to efforts at change. The value of academic affluence is widely accepted, at least by faculty members, but faculty behavior patterns are in conflict with the value pattern. And the doctrine of political neutrality is seriously questioned.

These conflicts within the academic community cannot be easily or soon resolved. They might be lessened in intensity with some evidence of social progress in meeting the problems of poverty, pollution, war and racism. It is also possible that these social circumstances and power conflicts, both within and without the academic community, will be with us for many years to come. We shall have to learn to live with them, or higher education as we have known it in our country will be destroyed by them.

VALUE PATTERNS AND POWER CONFLICT IN AMERICAN HIGHER EDUCATION

John D. Millett
Chancellor
Ohio Board of Regents

My assignment as I understand it is to provide an "over-view" or general analysis of the value patterns and power conflicts within the individual colleges and universities which comprise American higher education. I understand that in succeeding sessions you will explore these same value patterns and power conflicts in more detail from the point of view of various group participants in the struggle for power: faculty, students, and administration. You will also be examining the public interest and minority interest in the activities and operation of higher education.

The University As An Organized Entity

It is well to begin with some understanding of an institution of higher education as an organized entity, as an enterprise. One of the great dangers of our time is the tendency for so many people to see a college or university from a narrow personal or group perspective. In the conflicts of our day, power seems to transcend purpose, and group advantage appears to be more important than consensus. There is a crying need to understand higher education in its broadest concept, to comprehend its entire dimension.

One reason why a university is so vulnerable to attack, so helpless when caught in the turmoil of strife, is simply that so few persons are prepared to defend the university as a whole, as an organized entity. Faculties are not accustomed to think of the

1

university as an enterprise. In many universities the faculties of the various colleges and schools seldom, if ever, meet together, let alone consider common institutional concerns. Faculty representative bodies, such as a faculty senate or a faculty council, are more apt to view each concern in terms of their immediate constituency rather than in terms of the entire enterprise. In this sense, such bodies operate in the traditional mode of the legislative bodies with which we are familiar in our political society.

Just as it is the executive power in our political system which is expected to see our local and state governments and our federal government in their entirety, so it is our top-administrative staff of a university—the president and his immediate vice-presidential associates—who alone tend to see the enterprise as a whole. This situation seems to result in attitudes and behavior which place the burden of institutional defense upon the administrative staff, and which leave faculty members free individually to criticize but seldom to act effectively in crisis or in concert.

Meaning of Academic Freedom

Another reason why a university is vulnerable to attack is the devotion of the enterprise to academic freedom. Unfortunately, like so many phrases which become slogans and even battle cries, academic freedom is a concept subject to many interpretations. The appropriate meaning is relatively simple and restrictive.

Academic freedom means the privilege of a university faculty member to teach and to study as he personally deems appropriate. The obligation which is the obverse of this freedom—all freedoms in society entail both privileges *and* duties—is the responsibility to teach and study in ways recognized as academic. There is no point in identifying academic freedom as distinct from the regular civil freedoms of our constitutional system of government unless the word "academic" has some special importance. That importance is the privilege and the obligation to exercise one's freedom in the academic matters of teaching and studying in an academic manner.

Academic freedom is in large part accepted today in the United States. Difficulties tend to arise primarily when academic personnel stretch the cloak of academic freedom to deny accountability for statements made in the public forum, whether it be the public platform or the public press. Moreover, the difficulty is compounded when critics demand that the accountability for public statements be exercised by separation of the offending individual from his academic duties and by the denial of his academic freedom. Public accountability for free speech has been particularly troublesome to define and to enforce in our country. It is unfortunate, nonetheless, that freedom of speech which is a civil freedom seems always to get caught up in arguments about academic freedom when freedom of speech is exercised by an academic person.

Because a university is devoted to academic freedom, it protects and even encourages a wide range of points of view about academic subjects and about the academic enterprise. The expression of conflicting and critical points of view, the resolution of these points of view on academic subjects by the test of logical reasoning, and the resolution of these points of view on the academic enterprise through a process of consensus are the vital procedures of a university. When the expression of conflicting and critical points of view moves from the method of discussion to the methods of confrontation, disruption, and violence, the university is in trouble. Unfortunately, many persons inside a university seem unable to identify the point in time and action when expression becomes confrontation, a confrontation destructive of the academic enterprise itself.

Power Conflicts Within the University: Major Areas of Concern

This excursion into the organizational and procedural niceties of the academic enterprise may seem somewhat far afield from an analysis of value patterns and power conflicts. Yet if we are to understand conflict within a university, we must at the same time comprehend the peculiarities of structure and process which characterize the academic enterprise. These peculiarities help to compound the complexities of handling power conflicts within the university.

As I have reflected about the value patterns and the power conflicts which are prevalent within a university today, I have

3

identified four major areas of concern. Two of these have to do with the avowed and the actual objectives of the academic enterprise, and two have to do with operation of the enterprise. I label these areas of concern as:

1. The interaction of professions and of professional education.

2. The tradition of liberal education, or of humane learning.

3. The expectation of academic affluence.

4. The doctrine of institutional neutrality in social conflict.

Basic Mission of the Academic Enterprise

It seems to me that, above all other reasons, the most important single explanation of why universities are in trouble today is the absence of a clearly defined, explicit, and accepted mission for the academic enterprise. If the objective of the university is uncertain and confused, is it any cause for wonder that the university is beset by conflicts? The situation today is that many faculty members within a university do not accept the basic purpose of a university, and now that a generation of students has appeared, many of whose articulate spokesmen seek explanation of this basic purpose, some faculty members and some students are united in determination to alter that mission.

Let me state emphatically and unequivocally that the basic mission of a university in our society is professional education, the educational preparation of youth of appropriate talent to staff the professions of our society. Moreover, let me assert that such professional education historically has always been the basic mission of the university as we have known this institution in western culture since the twelfth century university in Bologna, Paris, and Oxford. I cannot take the time to mass the historical evidence to sustain this historical proposition. I can only assert that any objective scholar examining the record will be hard pressed, I believe, to arrive at any other conclusion.

The essential element in professional education is obviously the identification of the professions in society which require professional education for their practice. Another important element, of

4

course, is the determination of the content of what shall be deemed appropriate education for a profession; that is, what combination of specialized learning, humane learning, experience, and demonstrated skill shall be considered necessary for qualification to engage in professional practice.

One key factor in understanding America's achievements in economic growth, technological development, and social advancement has been the ever widening scope of our professions, and the ever expanding demand for professional talent. Undoubtedly there have been other influential factors in these achievements: the nation's climate and natural resources, the nature of the nation's immigrant population, the rewards to individual initiative, the ethic of work, the constitutional system, and the tradition of equality of opportunity. But surely near the head of any such listing must be the practical interaction of education and work, a practical interaction which was early noted and reported by De Tocqueville and other observers.

The Tradition of Classical Education

The classical tradition of higher education was brought by our colonial forebearers to these shores as the appropriate educational preparation for men to become ministers and lawyers. In the young republic of Andrew Jackson's day, classical education was opened to women, and then gradually classical education began to give way to more practical professional education. The scope of professions began to embrace school teaching, engineering, nursing, agricultural science, and then later architecture, journalism, business management, dentistry, pharmacy, optometry, and many others. Furthermore, certain long accepted professions became highly formalized insofar as educational preparation was concerned and were institutionalized in the university or the separate professional school; these professions included theology, law, medicine, and the profession of scholarship itself.

Moreover, professional talent was much in economic demand. Not only was the individuality of personal effort retained in such professions as medicine, law, and architecture, but also more and more institutions arose seeking the services of professionally educated persons. Government and the church have always been consumers of professional talent since the days of the University of Bologna and the University of Paris. But now the business corporation needed the engineer, the professional manager and his staff associates, and then scientists. The public school needed teachers. Government became a major employer of foresters, agricultural specialists, public health doctors, military officers, engineers, and later social workers and scientists, not to mention accountants and lawyers. An expanding higher education needed additional teacher-scholars. The end is not in sight.

Because professional education in seventeenth and eighteenth century England was a classical education, the kind of education then deemed appropriate for a landed aristocracy expected to govern in a constitutional monarchy, the United States inherited this classical education practice and began at once to adapt its content and process to the realities of the New World. Amazingly, we have retained down to our present day a goodly part of the tradition of that classical education within our American colleges and universities. We have retained this tradition in spite of changing circumstances and changing realities. This classical tradition is with us yet, whether we identify its content as the liberal arts, general education, or humane learning.

Competing Objectives

Let us note more specifically the nature of the value pattern and power conflict involved in these competing objectives of professional education and humane learning. Professional education seeks to provide educated talent for the application of knowledge to the "stubborn facts," as Alfred North Whitehead once labelled them, of man's society, his biological existence, and his physical environment. Professions involve the use of knowledge, the art of skilled performance, and the commitment to human betterment. Professions tend to become highly organized, so-called voluntary associations which set standards of professional conduct, seek to enforce observance of a code of ethics, promote interchange of experience, determine qualifications for entry into the profession, and influence the educational preparation for professional practice. Inevitably, professions tend to acquire certain common behavioral characteristics of a fairly cohesive

6

social grouping: to be defensive of accepted membership, to be more concerned about the welfare of the group than the welfare of others, and to be skeptical of any rapid social change.

The economic contribution of professions is substantial indeed in the American economy, even though any precise measurement is difficult to determine. It is customary in our national income accounting to speak of the production of goods and services, which is at least a recognition that vocational and professional services are a contribution to our national output along with goods. We have some idea about the value of certain professional services, such as banking and finance, health care, and education. We have little idea about the value of engineering, scientific, and management services which are a component element of our output of producers' and consumers' goods, our space exploration, and our national defense. It is safe to say, as have a number of economists in recent discussions, that a substantial part of our economic growth is the consequence of professional service rather than solely the result of new capital formation and of an expanding labor supply.

It seems to me unfortunate that professional education should be so widely misunderstood and so widely criticized by so many persons within our various academic professions. Somehow, for reasons which escape my comprehension, there are faculty members educated in the classical tradition who seem to think that professional education is personally demeaning, or intellectually second-rate. These persons appear to believe that the purpose of education is to cultivate the academic talents of an intellectual elite, to develop educational ability as a personal adornment and not as a social utility. These persons seldom know anything about the historical development of the classical tradition in higher education, its social role, or its economic context. These persons tend to think of higher education as enabling a few persons of outstanding intellectual ability to converse with one another; this appears to be sufficient social justification for its endeavor.

More recently, there is a new inclination evident among humanists, social scientists, and even biological and physical scientists steeped in the classical educational tradition. To these persons, learning is not enough just as an individual satisfaction.

7

Learning has a critical function to perform. Since knowledge is always partial, fragmentary, and subject to correction in the light of new research and synthesis, the learned man must always be skeptical of any accepted truth or any conventional wisdom. But the critical function tends to go beyond mere skepticism. The critical function is extended to all social behavior which the individual intellectual is inclined to dislike. This social behavior may be economic, political, or inter-personal. This social behavior may evidence itself in corporation policies, national defense policies, or racial prejudice.

It would seem that the intellectual tradition would call for social criticism by university faculty members to be voiced in intellectual terms. Certainly the reasoning which underlies any particular economic, political, or social policy and practice deserves critical intellectual scrutiny. Moreover, an expanding knowledge about social behavior and about biological and physical processes may very well provide new ideas about desirable social and other activity. It is social criticism divorced from intellectual foundation, and it is social criticism as social action which brings conflict between the academic world and the larger society, and which produces internal power conflicts within the academic community between the intellectual purist and the intellectual social activist. I shall return to this concern in a moment.

Goals of Humane Learning

I believe it is no ·exaggeration to say that, in spite of the tradition of classical education, there is today no concept of purpose in humane learning and no accepted process for achieving such goals as may be tentatively and variously formulated. It is all well and good for the well known Harvard report on General Education in a Free Society to postulate objectives such as to think effectively, to communicate thought, to make relevant judgments, and to accept certain value commitments, including the intellectual commitments of a respect for learning and a tolerance of conflicting ideas of knowledge. The difficulty is that this formulation of goals is too abstract to have real meaning, and that no two faculty members are likely to agree about how to accomplish such goals. It is not without significance of the troubled state of humane learning to observe that a few years ago

Columbia University entrusted the preparation of a report on the reforming of general education to a committee of *one* faculty member.

Humane learning seeks to provide the student in higher education with certain kinds of knowledge and certain behavioral characteristics as a supplement, or even as a foundation, for his professional education. Humane learning is concerned with the intellectual tradition in western society. Humane learning is concerned with the scope of man's artistic and intellectual expressions of his identity, not just those emanating from western culture but those from other cultures of this world, and not just those of the dominant white culture of the United States but with those of the Afro-American culture as well.

Humane learning is concerned with the definition of knowledge, the social role of knowledge, the limitations of knowledge, and the procedure for advancement of knowledge. Even if these generalizations suggest a desirable set of objectives for humane learning, there would be almost no agreement among any group of academic personnel in any academic community about the appropriate procedure for achieving these purposes. And particularly there would be little agreement about how much time in an undergraduate education to devote to the general purposes of humane learning.

But if humane learning as subject matter content is difficult to define, imagine the complications when we turn to the affective characteristics of learning. Contrary to the prevailing academic beliefs of 40 and even 20 years ago, I think there is a general realization today within our academic communities that emotions, attitudes, and value judgments are an integral part of higher education. The intellectual life cannot be neatly separated from the affective life of an individual.

Attitudes influence intellectual concepts; value judgments necessarily determine behavior no matter how much that behavior is founded upon an intellectual base. Thanks in large part to the findings of the psychologists of our day, especially the psychologists concerned with students as whole persons, we know that youth are seeking emotional maturity and value commitments while striving for intellectual achievement. The complication in this process is that academic scholars are decidedly self-conscious when it comes to discussing emotions and values. Scholars properly fear dogmatic authority and yet have no satisfactory alternative guide to individual behavior based upon reason alone.

The sad truth is that the very academic persons who tend to give most enthusiastic lip service to the ideals of humane learning in practice usually turn out to be practitioners of professional learning. These persons are more interested in developing students as professionally competent literary critics, economists, sociologists, chemists, physicists, biologists, and mathematicians than they are interested in developing students with a broad background in humane learning. Academic scholars, like other professionals, display the human tendency to be more concerned about perpetuation of their own type than concerned to encourage learning for the sake of learning.

Student Criticism of Humane Learning

Moreover, the concept of humane learning has now come under attack from student activists. Over and over we hear the accusation that higher education is irrelevant. Interesting enough, this charge seldom specifies that teacher education, business management education, engineering education, medical education, legal education, economics education, biological education, chemistry education, or mathematics education is irrelevant. No such degree of particularization is to be found in the literature of student protest, which I have read with some care. Rather, it appears that higher education in general, and this must mean general education or humane learning, is irrelevant to the interests and needs of many students in the current generation.

I believe my interpretation is not too far afield, since I have had students in various conferences say to me: "Sure, I want higher education in preparation for a job. But I want something more than a meal ticket from my higher education." I find this attitude disappointing for two reasons. First, this kind of attitude seems to suggest that work is a purely incidental and not a major concern of society and of the individual. Secondly, this attitude ignores the immense challenges of participation in a profession, including the

10

challenge of trying to accomplish effective change in society through professional channels. But in spite of these naive assumptions about professionalism, the students who want "something more" in their educational experience are surely struggling toward some current concept and practice of humane learning.

The student criticism of higher education appears to suggest that humane learning is too much concerned with man in the abstract and too little concerned with man's experience in today's society. Student criticism insists that humane learning must provide answers *now* to problems such as those of poverty, race relations, peace, and personal identification. If the humane learning avoids such answers, it is irrelevant. It is not enough to point out the limited scope of current knowledge and the partial role of knowledge in current social and individual behavior. It is not enough to suggest that students are asking too much of knowledge, and are as anti-intellectual in their expectation of knowledge as others are in their derision of knowledge. Somehow the humane learning of our day must bridge the gap between the abstractions of knowledge and the concern of students with identity and experience.

I do not wish to be understood as saying that there is no student criticism of professional education. On the contrary, there is such criticism, although I believe it comes from a handful of student militants rather than from the more numerous student activists of our day. Those few who hold all of present-day society to be corrupt, decadent, and worthless obviously are opposed to the professional education necessary to maintain this society. These militant students clearly and correctly perceive that the readiest means to destroy this society is to destroy the higher education indispensable to the life of society. If one accepts the revolutionary rather than the evolutionary prospect for the society we know, then such an individual cannot readily accept professional education as we now know it.

Definition of Objectives: A Source of Conflict

In brief, it appears to me that there are major power conflicts within American higher education involving our definition of objectives. Value patterns among many scholars seem to inhibit

11

the acknowledgement that the major objective of American higher education is professional education, is the preparation of talent for meaningful and productive participation in the professional pursuits of American society. If we are reluctant to acknowledge this purpose, we are nonetheless vigorous in our pursuit of it. At the same time, within the academic community we are almost all of us loud in our declaration of loyalty to the concept of liberal education or humane learning, but exceedingly inept in any endeavor to give such purpose real meaning or process.

The two cultures of American higher education are professional education and humane learning. And the dominant culture is professional education. I do not criticize this circumstance; I deplore the value pattern which prevents our explicit recognition of this fact and which thereby generates a power conflict which is unnecessary and debilitating to the higher education enterprise. I deplore, also, our inability to develop a meaningful program of humane learning to supplement professional education. Perhaps the student activists of our day will make a major contribution in demanding some new attention and some new efforts at realizing the elusive objective of humane learning.

Quest for Faculty Affluence

An obvious value pattern within higher education is the desire for faculty affluence. In 1957 President Eisenhower's Committee on Education Beyond the High School declared that the "absolute highest priority" in the use of higher education funds should be given to the objective of doubling the average level of faculty salaries within ten years. The report of the committee gave the median faculty salary in the United States as $5,400 per year as of 1953-54, and indicated that the median salary for full professors that year was $7,000.

In 1968-69, according to the survey of the American Association of University Professors, the average salary of faculty members came to $11,760. This record was just about the doubling of salary levels proposed in 1957. Unfortunately, in this same period of time the consumer price index had advanced by almost 24 percent, so that in terms of dollars of constant

12

purchasing power the objective of doubling faculty salaries had not been achieved.

Continuously since 1957, various arguments have been advanced for increases in faculty salaries. The impact of inflation upon real income has been stressed many times. Comparisons of faculty salaries with other professional salaries have been utilized to indicate that higher education personnel are not adequately compensated. The importance of higher education to national security, to technological development, and to economic growth have been repeatedly emphasized.

I think it is fair to say that a major goal of higher education and of faculty members in the past 15 years has been a steady improvement in the compensation received for faculty instructional and other services. The difficulty has been that the complexities of financing higher education have hampered or frustrated this goal. As a result, still another kind of power conflict has developed within colleges and universities.

Higher education is financed in three ways: charges to students, appropriations by government, and philanthropic giving. Faculty members are generally unlikely to advocate within the college or university where they serve that students ought to pay more for their education. Not only are decisions about available income left primarily to administrative officers and boards of trustees, but also in some way administrative officers are expected to obtain the maximum possible income from government and from benefactors. This expectation is often undermined by the refusal of faculty members to contribute in any effective way to these fund-raising efforts on the part of administrative officers.

The contrast between faculty attitudes and value patterns concerning research and those concerning instruction are quite remarkable. In the past 30 years and even more, faculty members have generally understood that grants in support of their research interests had to be obtained primarily on their own. The individual faculty member developed his own research ideas and procedures, made a market survey of foundations, and then later of federal government agencies likely to be interested in the project, explained the reasons to research project evaluators (usually his

13

own peers) why his particular project deserved financial support, and then proceeded to carry out the project if and when the requested funds were made available. University research to a very considerable degree has been a matter of individual or team entrepreneurship. The university as an enterprise was simply the convenient vehicle for assisting the researcher to carry out his research interests.

Contrast, if you will, this position of fiscal initiative and endeavor evident in the research field with the attitude of faculty members when the instructional expenses and income of a college or university are at stake. The customary attitude of faculty members is that administrators (including trustees) shall fix the instructional charges made to students, shall present the case to chief executives and legislators for increased government appropriations, and shall cajole gifts from alumni, corporations, wealthy individuals, and any other source of funds. Faculty members as individuals and as a group have evidenced almost no interest in helping administrators to convince political representatives of the people to spend more money for higher education or to cultivate donations from potential benefactors.

Needed: A Favorable Public Image

Worse than this. Faculty behavior in accordance with the value patterns which stress academic freedom and social criticism is often in conflict with administrative efforts to obtain more income for the instructional and other needs of the academic enterprise. Government officials must be persuaded that higher education is fulfilling a major social need as recognized by the political process if they are to provide increased appropriations in support of colleges and universities.

The voting public as influenced by interest groups and by the media of mass communication must also be supportive if executives and legislators are to increase taxes and are to appropriate larger sums of money for the benefit of higher education.

All of this means that faculty members and students as well as administrators must establish and maintain a favorable public

14

image if increased financial support for higher education is to be obtained from government.

The same considerations apply to the effort to obtain funds for higher education through philanthropic channels. Individuals of considerable wealth, alumni and friends of moderate means, corporation executives, and foundation officials must be persuaded that there is some particularly good reason why each one should provide some part of his income earmarked for charitable giving to the higher education enterprise.

The corporate executive may be persuaded that his business benefits by the recruitment of talent from higher education, from the research and consulting services provided by higher education, or from the neighboring proximity of a particular college or university. The alumni may be persuaded that alma mater still needs financial assistance even as this was given when each alumnus or alumna was a student. The foundation official may be persuaded that some new ideas or new efforts in higher education will be realized from a particular contribution. The philanthropist may be persuaded that no charity brings greater individual satisfaction or more enduring social benefit than a gift to a college or university.

These efforts at political and personal persuasion may be set back when faculty members and students become more interested in social criticism than in social contribution, more interested in finding fault with conventional attitudes than in counteracting these attitudes with appeals to enlightened self-interest. Faculty members want the public and the philanthropist to underwrite their enlarged sharing in the affluence of the American economy. Students want the public and the philanthropist to contribute to the expense of their educational efforts. But the winning of friends and the influencing of people is considered a chore fit only for administrators. Is such cultivation beneath the dignity and integrity of academic man and inconsistent with the escape from parental authority which is the preoccupation of the undergraduate student?

How then are the salaries of faculty members to be increased in proportion with or in excess of the rate of growth for professional incomes generally? Faculty members in the academic community have no answer to this question. Indeed, it is surprising how seldom faculty members even ask the question. Yet salary affluence is the expectation of every faculty member. The administrator asks faculty members to help him "sell" higher education. The request is largely ignored. Yet faculty members ask the administrator continuously to increase their compensation. From this remarkable pattern of value judgments flows a never-ending stream of power conflicts within higher education.

Social Neutrality vs. Social Involvement

There is a newly emerging power conflict evident today in the disposition of student activists and some faculty members to question the political role of higher education. I believe it is reasonable and accurate to say that the traditional value pattern of higher education has asserted a role of political neutrality amid the competing interests and conflicts of society. The university undertook to provide the professional talent needed by society. The university conserved an intellectual tradition of inquiry, speculation, and criticism. The university might be called upon for special services and advice; these were rendered as requested and as consistent with university purposes without taking sides among competing groups in society.

Higher education has conceived of itself as simply one among various social institutions. Higher education has a special social function to fulfill as just enumerated. But higher education has not ordinarily thought of itself as a participant in the power conflicts of society, the economy, the polity, and religion. Higher education is not synonymous with the family, with a community, with an ethnic group, a voluntary association, a political party. Higher education is not synonymous with a professional practitioner, an individual proprietorship, a business firm, or a corporation. Higher education is not synonymous with a municipality, a township, a county, a state, or the federal government. Higher education is not synonymous with any denominational church, with any agnostic group, with any person or group proclaiming atheism. Toward all these various institutional arrangements in society higher education has traditionally maintained a certain aloofness, a certain reserve.

16

Today there are persons and groups within the academic enterprise who do not accept the concept of a university as a center of learning. Instead, they conceive of the university as an instrument of social power, as a direct participant in political and social controversy.

These persons argue that society as now organized and as it now operates evidences a number of basic faults. Socially, some persons endure poverty and hunger, blacks suffer racial discrimination, urban communities are congested and polluted, health care is unevenly distributed, educational opportunity is unequal. The economy is dominated by large corporations which must make a profit to survive, which consume natural resources without concern for conservation or replacement, and which ignore human needs. The political system is diffuse and beyond popular control. Bureaucracy is slow, ponderous, inflexible, nonresponsive to changing circumstances. Foreign policy is dominated by the military-industrial complex which engages in wars overseas beyond the realm of American national interests. Religion is no longer of importance. These and similar arguments are to be heard on every campus throughout the land.

What is different today from previous years is not the argument, but the reaction to the argument. Student militants are saying that it is the proper task of the university in America to restructure a decadent, imperialist, racist, and immoral society. Student activists are proposing that higher education undertake projects to help urban communities, schools, the poor, and the disadvantaged. Some faculty members want the university to improve housing in the community and to provide counseling services to the non-academic personnel employed by the university. Some faculty members want the university to be a power instrument in the neighboring community, urging improvements in streets, sanitation, recreation, and other facilities. Such action is advocated even though colleges and universities generally do not pay general property taxes and so provide little, if any, direct income to the government of the community.

Obviously, demands upon higher education of the kind just outlined are based upon the concept of social involvement, not social neutrality. Moreover, higher education is expected to be an

17

instrument or agency of benevolent power, paternalistically deciding what is best for the community and undemocratically imposing these decisions upon the community whether acceptable to a large proportion of the population or not. When one listens to the arguments for higher education to exercise political and social power, one wonders what kind of power structure and power process these advocates envisage for the "new" America.

It is not too difficult to see that the activist university as a social instrument would soon become rent with internal divisions among its faculty, students, and administrators for control of this power machine. It is not too difficult to see that those in society opposed to the policy positions of the university would seek to limit or destroy its power and certainly would object to providing funds for the financial support of such an active power bloc. It is not too difficult to see that the educational mission of the university would necessarily be subordinated to the social and political position of its power status. Other power groups and instruments in society—the corporation, the labor union, government agencies, churches—would be compelled to develop their own universities to provide the educated talent needed for survival. It is not too difficult to see that the university would lose any claim of service to society in general.

It is worth emphasizing that the role of political neutrality assumed by higher education is the one position which gives colleges and universities the opportunity to lay claim to support from society in general. No matter what the conflicts in society, no matter what the power struggles between corporations and unions, between churches and nonchurch groups or even between church denominations, between various voluntary associations, between rich and poor, between white and black, between political parties—no matter what the power struggle, higher education has remained uncommitted. As a social institution, higher education has said that it was aloof from these immediate conflicts and that the benefits of higher education in terms of educated talent, research, and public service were equally available to all groups, to all participants in the power struggle.

Yet it is obvious, I believe, that there are articulate individuals and groups within higher education who do not accept this

18

position of political neutrality. Certainly this position is not accepted by the Students for a Democratic Society and by the New University Conference. This position is not accepted by those faculty committees who at some universities now advocate that universities take an active role in community housing and in certain other community projects. It is not clear whether the full ramifications of these new thrusts have been carefully examined or not.

In any event, a traditional value pattern, the doctrine of political neutrality, is now being seriously questioned within higher education today, and this questioning is producing still another power conflict within the academic community between those who oppose and those who defend the position of political neutrality.

Criticisms of Traditional Value Patterns
Generate Power Conflicts

Higher education in the United States confronts students and faculty members who are criticizing present value patterns. The emphasis upon professional education is under attack. The ostensible commitment to humane learning is subject to two kinds of effort at change: to broaden the cultural base to include African or Afro-American culture and to alter the philosophical emphasis from intellectual abstraction to personal identity or social improvement. The value of academic affluence is widely accepted, at least by faculty members, but faculty behavior patterns are in conflict with the value pattern. And the doctrine of political neutrality is seriously questioned.

All of these criticisms of traditional value patterns give rise to basic power conflicts within higher education. The power base of these conflicts shifts with the particular issue under discussion. Students tend to be concerned with educational objectives, but somewhat lacking in concern about faculty affluence. Faculty members are divided among themselves on issues of educational purpose and process, strongly committed to academic affluence, but indifferent to the means for maintaining and advancing that affluence. Students and faculty members are divided among themselves about the utility and desirability of the doctrine of political neutrality.

These conflicts within the academic community will not be easily or soon resolved. These conflicts might be lessened in intensity with some evidence of social progress in meeting the problems of poverty, pollution, war, and racism. It is possible that these conflicts have been intensified by present social circumstances. But it is also possible that these social circumstances and power conflicts, both within and without the academic community, will be with us for many years to come. We shall have to learn to live with them, or higher education as we have known it in our country will be destroyed by them.

Precis

The brief but hectic weeks of the Danforth Foundation Workshop on Liberal Education, in which I have participated the past two summers, provide a useful synopsis of recent events in the American academy. The depth and intensity of disagreement among workshop participants are indicative of developing power conflicts within universities and colleges today.

During the past year, there has been a general hardening of opinions and attitudes in every stratum of the university—the "left," "right," and "center." Members of the academy who are satisfied with the existing organization of the university are far more determined than they were a year ago to protect it. This fact is reflected in their increasing acceptance of violence and repression as indispensable adjuncts of educational policy.

All of the major power conflicts within the academy seem to turn on the question of its structure. Some of these conflicts concern the structure of the university as an end in itself. However, many other supposed disagreements over structure are ways of concealing disagreements over basic educational policy and purpose. Many students and faculty demand increasing power in university governance precisely in order to modify the ends now pursued by the academic establishment.

These dissidents argue that the university must assume new social functions and roles rather than confine itself to the traditional roles of teaching, learning and study. They believe that only by accepting an enlarged sense of its educational and social missions can the university justly claim a position of centrality in today's society.

The conflicts of power within the academy reflect wider conflicts of power and patterns of value in the national society. The deep malaise of the university is related to our country's inability to conclude a futile, debilitating war in the Far East and to the unwillingness of our affluent society to cope effectively with its domestic disorders.

The power conflicts both on the campus and in the society have made it clear that, unless we academicians display more care both for the protection and the enlightenment of all our kind, including our dissenting students and faculty, our sacred academy will not be worth saving.

22

HOW LATE IS IT?

Henry David Aiken
Professor of Philosophy
Brandeis University

I have had the rather special benefit of participating the past two summers as a seminar leader at the Danforth Foundation Workshop on Liberal Education at Colorado College.[1] The brief but hectic weeks of the Danforth workshop provide a useful synopsis, as well as simulacrum, of the drift of events in the American academy, as well as in the social order—or disorder—of whose health the academy has become at once a sensitive symptom and a determining cause. All the more impressive, therefore, are the astonishing changes in temper and in attitude which I have discovered among the membership of this workshop in the space of one academic year.

In 1968, when no students were participating members and no black teacher was a seminar leader, serious divisions of opinion existed within the workshop. But, as yet, no conflicts of attitude emerged which precluded belief in a residual consensus about the ends of higher education; the essential worth of the academic establishment, despite its many obvious limitations and faults; or the benefits to be derived from an education in any of our great national universities.

In 1969, a few students were added to our ranks, and although the small number of black teachers among our lay-membership remained about the same, we acquired a particularly brilliant and dedicated black professor as a seminar leader. In general, however, the composition of the membership was not radically different from what it had been in previous years. But this year, not only was there a sense of mounting tension throughout the workshop rising in some instances to open hostility, but more significantly, there was little common faith in the reality of a working consensus either about the values and aims of higher learning or about the forms of organization and governance proper to an acceptable university. Often, old colleagues and friends were barely on speaking terms, and efforts to conclude the workshop with at least an appearance of mutual confidence and good will were largely unsuccessful.

Some depreciated the significance of these oppositions. Others sought to "cool it," either by pretending that the divisions didn't exist; suggesting that they did not really involve any considerable number of the workshop membership; or by reminding us that, after all, life at the workshop is brief and their commitment to it relatively low, at least in their own order of academic priorities. But such efforts to minimize the importance of the changes in character which the academic experience of one year had wrought in the life of the workshop were, in my opinion, unavailing. In fact, precisely because we were a varied and carefully selected group of teachers, administrators, and students, the depth and intensity of our disagreements must be of the very greatest interest to anyone concerned with the significance of existing power conflicts within universities and colleges and their relations to prevailing patterns of value in our society.

Developing Power Conflicts

Employing my experience at the Danforth workshop, let me define some of the shifts in the developing power conflicts within the academy and in the educational and sociopolitical outlooks which I have observed among my fellow academicians during the past year. I shall also try to relate these changes to developments within the larger society that may reflect correlative changes in our national value patterns.

Many more of us are now aware that, throughout our system of higher education, time is rapidly running out. While we continue to believe in the virtues of rationality, reflectiveness, and impartiality, we are obliged by the ominous circumstances to come directly to terms with the great issues that confront us. These issues include:

1. Student participation in the educational and administrative affairs of the academy.

2. The peremptory demands of black people for studies that reflect their own interests and their own historic experience within a predominantly white country.

3. The incursions into the universities and colleges of increasing numbers of "disadvantaged" students, ill-prepared for the highly technical studies now required for professional competence in most disciplines.

4. The precipitous decline of liberal education and the correlative demand on the part of the dissident groups for better, updated, more relevant studies concerned with the problems of men in contemporary society.

5. The unsatisfactory quality of life in the academy, not only for student and faculty radicals who employ unconventional means to secure their ends, but also for conservative faculty members and administrators whose subservience to the "military-industrial" complex is now criticized by their fellow academicians.

6. The predicaments of the urban university in an environment which is hostile to its traditional educational activities and forces it to reconsider and to reconstruct those activities virtually at a moment's notice.

7. The pervasive awareness of malaise throughout the academy and the consequent speculations about the academy's sheer will and power to survive in a society in which many of the tasks of professional and technical education can be as well or better performed in the para-educational institutes and laboratories now maintained by industry and government.

Everywhere the time available for deliberation appears to be radically foreshortened, and scholars, like everyone else, find that they must make the best of it. On the more positive side, however, they now increasingly recognize time as a *value* in its own right whose exigent demands can no longer be postponed indefinitely.

Violence and Repression

I am impressed by the general hardening of opinions and attitudes in every stratum of the university—the "left," "right," and "center." Those who are satisfied with the existing organization of the university and with the correlative roles, functions, and ends which that organization implements, are now far more determined than they were even a year ago to protect it. This fact is reflected in their increasing readiness to resort to the overwhelming power of civil and legal authorities, even at the expense of the cherished principle of academic extraterritoriality, in order to put down forms of student and faculty supported protest that directly threaten the organizational *status quo*.

The fact is reflected in their increasing acceptance of violence or counter-violence as indispensable adjuncts of educational policy. Whereas violence had hitherto been decreasingly accepted as part of the educational process, it is now taken for granted as a necessity, especially within the precincts of the higher learning itself. In short, violence and repression are no longer generally regarded as primary disvalues in the academy. In the eyes of many realists, violence is now construed as a positive support of "rationality" itself, just as many radicals have contended since the time of Karl Marx.

Challenge to Authority

The same point may be made even more saliently in terms of the concept of authority. The "conservatives," as I shall call them, are increasingly impatient with radical students and faculty members who challenge on principle the prevailing provenance and governance of the university. In their efforts to maintain their own authority and power positions within it, they find themselves increasingly alienated from large segments not only of the student body but also of the faculty and, in some instances, the administration.[2] To this extent they become, in spite of themselves, symbols of repression to their critics. For the same reason

26

they are regarded by their adversaries as primary sources of violence or counter-violence, determined to maintain their own established positions at any cost.

Because the formal authority of trustees and, behind them, the legislatures has been so readily reconverted into peremptory actual power, that authority is automatically challenged by its victims. Indeed, the latter are commonly driven, however mistakenly and futilely, into anarchistic positions which impugn any form of authority, and especially of external authority, on principle. The movement symbolized by the phrase "participatory democracy" can in part be construed, both on the campus and outside it, as a counter-response to a misapplied and diversive authority whose actions are now interpreted by dissidents as little more than a naked display of arbitrary institutional power.

The authority and power of trustees and, behind them, legislatures must in daily practice be largely delegated to academic administrators, including not only presidents and deans but also department heads and senior committee men. Accordingly, the latter find themselves caught between their colleagues and students, with whose attitudes and conduct they often personally sympathize, and the still higher authorities whose agents and representatives they are. Unfortunately, the administrators appear to their critics no longer as honest middle-men and negotiators, but rather as servants of the powers to whom they owe their office.

This fact serves to exacerbate the sense of misunderstanding and alienation between the administration and many senior faculty on the one side and students and junior faculty on the other. On both sides questions of "priority" become increasingly exigent. Opponents of the existing "system" demand that its exponents fish or cut bait; in their own foreshortened view, those who are not "with us" are "against us." On the other side, exponents of the system, whatever their private reservations, are now obliged to give first priority to the "defense" of the existing university, along with its authority and power structures, and hence to view all deep criticism as evidence of institutional disaffection.

The increasing determination of university leaders and spokesmen to preserve and to protect the existing university as an institution *ipso facto* increases the prevailing conflicts. Influential exponents of the prevailing system, such as McGeorge Bundy, are ridiculed when they tell us that the real authority and power of the university resides, as they believe it should, in "the faculty." For the same reason, those who contend that the power of trustees is merely formal are regarded as hypocritical sycophants. The ready reactivation of that formal power in critical situations makes clear, at least to those against whom it is directed, where the real power within the academy actually lies.

The Dissenting Academy

Rigidity breeds rigidity, just as violence breeds counter-violence, and the exercise of power creates its own opposition. It is no accident that just as the attitudes of the conservative forces within the university have hardened, so have those of their adversaries. In a classic sense of the term, we are now witnesses to an all too real "agon" whose dialectic must be understood before it can begin to be resolved. Disaffected students now present nonnegotiable demands.[3] Dissenting faculty members condemn their colleagues and the administrators whom the latter defend. The occasional administrator who is determined at all costs to preserve the principle of extraterritoriality on the campus, even if this means allowing infractious students to occupy university buildings indefinitely, is obliged to resign.

However, necessity creates strange bed-fellows. Those who are prepared finally to stand on a principle find that their own priorities force them, often against their will, into the camp of the dissenters of whom they may otherwise disapprove. The principled administrator or faculty member sometimes finds himself drawn into the ranks of the radically dissenting academy. In the same way, the dissenting academy itself becomes by stages a rebellious academy, some of whose members are now girding themselves to accept the demise of their own institutions for the sake of what they esteem to be its proper educational ideals.

Thus the range of negotiable issues, or the willingness to negotiate, has plainly diminished during the past year. And those who are still committed to the principle of negotiation (which they sometimes mistakenly identify with rationality itself) are caught in a no-man's land between opposing activists. Of these, not many have moved by stages into the camp of the dissidents. More frequently they find themselves drawn in spite of themselves into the camp of hardened conservatives who contend that the time for negotiation is now passed and who are prepared to call in the police at 15 minutes notice to clear their campuses of obstructors. Thus, by a tragic irony, professors of reason and argument find themselves committed in practice to the use of pre-emptive academic, legal, and political power in order to force the dissidents to "listen to reason." And their resort to force in turn makes the latter ever more intransigent.

I am not saying here that we have actually reached a point of no return within the dissenting and counter-dissenting academy. Nor do I profess to know where such a point lies. But everywhere there is an increasing sense that it now lies within the range of existing possibilities, and hence that irresolvable conflict within the universities and colleges may be an impending reality. Thus, as I discovered at the Danforth workshop this year, there exists on all sides a pervasive mood of stoical resignation regarding divisions of opinion and attitude.

In another way, those who still profess to believe in the fine old ideal of mutual trust and liberal consensus no longer strive ever more patiently to realize it in their own actions. In fact, those who talk of such things as "trust" and "community" commonly seem ever more abstract and remote from the actualities of university life. As it turns out, unfortunately, their own conduct constantly belies their ideals. They yearn for community, but act in ways that diminish the possibility of significant communities of attitude and feeling. They nostalgically recall the good old times when there was a deep underlying trust among students, faculty, and administration. But in practice they are no less mistrustful of their colleagues, their students, or their academic superiors than those dissidents who tell each other that there are none to trust any longer but themselves and a few like-minded spirits.

29

Conflicts Over University Structure

All of the major power conflicts within the academy seem to turn on the question of its structure. However, all of these conflicts are not of the same sort. Initially, at least, it seems possible to range them under two main heads. Whether they can all be so classified is unclear. Indeed, it is by no means certain whether in the end even these types of conflict are themselves distinct.

Structure as Means to an End

The first type of conflict concerning the existing structure of the university does not appear at first to involve basic disagreements about the ultimate aims of the higher learning. For example, many students who demand greater participation in the governance of the university, especially in matters of appointments and curriculum, often seem initially to share with their elders the same broad attitudes concerning the aims of the higher learning.

Thus I have found very few student activists who deny that the university should concern itself with the advancement of learning, through teaching and research, in all the main departments of human inquiry and culture. They may demand that more of their teachers' time be devoted to teaching, but few deny that regular independent study is essential to successful teaching, and that without such study teachers become drudges and hacks.

Moreover, not many student activists, in my experience, deny the importance to themselves of rigorous preprofessional and professional studies arranged around a field of major interest. They merely insist that such studies take into account all relevant contemporary phenomena and that they be effectively integrated with comprehensive studies that place them securely and discriminatingly within the wiser contexts of human life and culture.

A very considerable majority of their elders very likely share this view, however obsessed they may become in practice with their own professional investigations and activities. The drifts toward professionalism, specialism, and scientism in the university seem not to be matters of individual intent, but of institutional factors both within the academy and the society which put a high premium upon professional distinction and which accordingly direct tendencies toward competitiveness and emulation into increasingly narrow channels of inquiry. The prevailing systems of institutional and social rewards and penalties make it difficult, even for men committed in principle to a more liberal conception of higher education, consistently to act in accordance with their beliefs. It is precisely for this reason that many student activists oppose existing patterns of academic organization. For the same reason these students are likely to be political and social radicals who demand corresponding structural changes in other institutions within our society.

Many faculty members, including especially junior members, who demand wider faculty participation in the basic decision-making processes of the university, do not seem at first to differ radically either from the trustees, the administration, or their more compliant colleagues concerning what President James Perkins of Cornell calls the primary "missions" of the university— instruction, research, and public service. They complain rather about their own incapacity to play a continuing and decisive part in establishing policies designed to implement such missions or ends. Their complaint is based upon the contention that the trustees, the administrators, and senior research professors, largely responsible to themselves or their own superiors, continually subvert the very ends which they profess. Once more the assumption is that existing structures of authority and power preclude forms of effective participation and review on the part of the faculty at large that might result in policies more consonant with the proper missions of the academy.

According to the present hypothesis, dissident students and faculty members demand a restructuring of the university in ways that would give them more effective power only because they believe, rightly or wrongly, that the existing modes of governance within the university make it difficult or impossible to implement the professed purposes for which the academy exists. But such a view of the matter is superficial. For when such conflicts over the existing structure of the university are more deeply probed, it soon becomes evident that the consensus concerning the ends of

31

the university described above is abstract and unreal. It is simply not true, in the view of more thoughtful dissenting members of the academy, that substantive agreement concerning the ends of higher education any longer exists.

For example, many students demand a greater role in the decision-making process because they consider the existing curriculum, especially in the social sciences, history, and the humanities, largely irrelevant to their own historical predicaments and their social and cultural aspirations both as students and as human beings. And faculty members are profoundly repelled by prevailing conceptions of public service according to which they themselves are expected to participate. Many are angered by the ties between the university as an institution and the governmental-military-industrial complexes. They condemn academic practices that, in effect, place the facilities of the university, including its faculties, at the disposal of institutions of whose own goals and policies they passionately disapprove.

To shrewder members of the dissenting academy it begins to appear that supposed disagreements over structure are frequently ways of concealing disagreements over basic educational policy and purpose which in their view should be debated in their own terms. They demand increasing power precisely in order to modify the ends now pursued by the academic establishment.

Structure as an End in Itself

The second type of power conflict within the university mentioned above also concerns questions of governance and organization. But it does not at first glance seem to be concerned with issues about the ulterior ends of higher education. At least some of the power conflicts seem to concern the structure of the university as an end in itself. Thus some students oppose the existing structure because it excludes them from effectual control over university affairs. Like their elders, whom they not unnaturally emulate, they also want to run things and are disgruntled when they cannot do so. The will to domination is very strong in a society such as ours, and those excluded from the corridors of power often contest the order which excludes them merely because it leaves them out. In some instances the profession of supposedly higher motives appears to be nothing more than a mask.

However, many students and faculty members demand a restructuring of the university which will give them greater power in the determination of its policies for better reasons. They sincerely believe that their own presence on the governing boards and committees of the university will of itself insure a better chance for a genuine community of scholars. They argue that the application of the principle of participatory democracy, or community, within the classrooms, within archaic self-serving academic departments, as well as within the over-arching administration of the university is a positive human good, desirable on its own account. As I understand, what they demand and are prepared to fight for is, in sum, a truer polity or city of the mind within the academy so that all its members may better fulfill themselves as liberated human beings.

For much the same reason, academic dissidents also demand basic structural changes in the governance of the university which will, in their opinion, radically reduce the psychological distances that prevail among members of the major classes within the university. From their point of view, such forms of psychological distance are both symptoms and causes of human alienation which are inherently devisive and destructive. Nor are they content with the reply that some forms of psychological distance and alienation may be necessary or even desirable in the university as elsewhere, for indispensable divisions of labor, differentiations of function, and accompanying systems of authority.

Stated in these terms, those who accept such a reply as sufficient remind one of conservative Catholics within the Christian church, just as their opponents remind one of radical Protestants who regard the historical church as paradoxically corruptive of all who aspire to live a Christian life. Similarly, the former remind us of those who, in more obvious political terms, maintain that even within a liberal democracy, established aristocratic principles of hierarchy and authority are necessary to the administration of justice, just as their opponents remind us of classical revolutionists who contend that the only just polity must be one of institutional liberty, equality, and fraternity.

Conflict Over University Function

Once such analogies come in view, another issue that divides members of the academy is forced upon us. "Strict constructionists" like to remind us that the university is essentially a place for teaching, learning, and study. They are fond of telling us that the university is not and cannot properly serve as a church or state. They warn us that, unless the university limits its conception of its functions, it will involve itself unnecessarily and at great cost in wider political and social conflicts that are not and cannot be its concern. Accordingly, they accept the fact that the university, like the legal system, is an institution which can no longer be, or pretend to serve as, a community either of scholars or of men.

This contention has strength. Yet it fails to satisfy dissenting "loose constructionists" for whom the university must now assume historic social functions and roles whose importance short-sighted formalists fail to appreciate. The former contend that in an era of prolonged cultural crisis, when other institutions are no longer adequate to their occasions as carriers of central social and human values, the university is obliged to assume at least some of the functions of a church or a polity. They believe that only by accepting such an enlarged sense of its educational and social missions can the university justly claim the position of centrality which its own functionaries themselves ascribe to it. Such a contention is easily misunderstood. It does not entail that ordinary officers of the university must in any literal sense assume the roles of priests or statesmen. Patently this gentry is unprepared for such roles.

What is asked for is an enlarged sense of the whole university's contemporary vocation as a repository of human culture and learning, a new determination on the part of academicians to serve as independent critics of manifest cultural confusions and institutional inversions, and, more generally, a readiness on their part to assume a more active role as "conscience" to the society. In the name of these roles and purposes, it is contended that the university must first clean its own house by cutting off its subservient services to the military establishment and its industrial adjuncts, and by assuming its proper and inescapable responsibilities for rehabilitation of the university city over which, in so many cases, it now presides as an oppressive landlord.

Undoubtedly students and faculty members who take this view tend to regard themselves, in effect, as a new "elect" (in the traditional Protestant sense of the term) which may serve as a carrier of a revived and relevant idealism to which their elders—the grantsmen, the vocationalists, the old-pros, and the pragmatists—now pay only reluctant lip service. It is not so much that their ideals are different from those professed by their elders. They mean in all seriousness, by their actions as well as by their words, to rejuvenate an imperial sociopolitical order, including its acquiescent academic knowledge factories and service stations. They understand, however, as did their Protestant forbearers, that they cannot fulfill their mission without power and hence, on occasion, without risking the possibility of violence. Jean-Paul Sartre wisely reminds us that such violence is always to be understood as a counter-violence or retaliation to the violence of "the Other."

Their critics, who are legion, charge these would-be Luthers with *hubris* or *chutzbah*. They call them romantics, utopians, chiliastic visionaries who would replace the university, with its traditional finite educational ends, with something else which in anticipation might gratify their own infinite yearnings for union and redemption but which is no longer a proper or manageable institution of patient study, research, and learning.

These critics, to whom I listened endlessly this year at the Danforth workshop, charge such dissident students and their faculty supporters with generating a sense of unstructured totalistic crisis which, because it is objectless and devoid of empirical content, is therefore incapable of meaningful resolution. In the name of justice, some of them admit to a certain admiration for the passion and courage of these "rejuvenators," as they may be called, but ridicule them for failing to provide any acceptable plan for orderly institutional and social change.

More generally, they charge such idealists with being both victims and manipulators of general ideas who lack the factual information required for predictable institutional improvements.

Other critics are even less generous. They imply that, like most other malcontents and incipient revolutionists, the underlying motivation of such academic idealists is sheer resentment. These dissidents, incapable of either instruction, discipline, or the exercise of authority essential to all great achievements of civilization, and lacking more useful outlets for their aggression, seek by any means at hand to humiliate their betters and to bring them down to their own wretched levels of unexamined protest and violence.

Perhaps there is something in this. Resentment, like aggression, is a universal sentiment, and when deprived access to an authority that continually works to our disadvantage, we all are subject to the destructive impulses it may occasion. Resentment, which is by no means always self-interested, also has another name: the sense of justice or reciprocity. And though resentful men may not understand the cause of their affliction, just as the man who demands justice may not always know how to realize it, they still deserve to be listened to.

Here use may be made of a striking medical analogy suggested to me at the Danforth workshop by Professor Donald Larsen of Texas. This is provided by the concept of "referred pain"; that is, pain which crops out in places that may be remote from the source of bodily disorder. Referred pain is not illusory even though it cannot be removed by remedies applied directly to the painful organ; rather it is an associated symptom of genuine and potentially lethal malfunctioning elsewhere in the organism. Something has gone wrong which must be located and remedied if the organism is to be restored to health.

Thus, what we have to consider, even if we do not accept at face-value the dissenters' descriptions of the source of evils either in the university or in the larger body-politic, is the quasi-"medical" question: what is it that *now* disposes them to acts of desperation in the absence of any one justifying cause? More generally, what are the deep-lying maladies in the organization and economy of our universities and colleges that result at this time in so many diverse forms of referred pain everywhere in the academy?

36

The Deep Maladies in Universities

The answer to such a question cannot be simple. A part of it undoubtedly concerns long-standing internal malfunctionings within the university. For example, we have now to reckon with the consequences of a hundred years of infatuation with the 19th century ideals of the German university, with its Ph.D. system and its rigid academic hierarchies of ordinary and extraordinary professors, its conscienceless commitment to "pure" research, and its indifference to the claims of liberal education which was henceforth delegated to the *gymnasium*.

Our own universities have indeed become knowledge factories dominated by graduate schools interested exclusively in forms of study and training necessary to specialized and professional scientific or parascientific inquiry. Accordingly, our universities and colleges are now institutes for the training of preprofessional and technological elites. And their faculties are themselves sytematically deprived of the forms of training and experience required for rehabilitating the entire university as an institution of relevant human learning. They themselves are victims of referred pain who are forced back in times of stress on conventional formulas for restoring order and continuity so that they can get on with their scientific and professional work.

In a larger sense the entire university is dominated by the baneful ideology of "rationalism" which puts a premium upon the theoretical-explanatory conception of knowledge and hence automatically downgrades all forms of understanding that do not conform to this model. The whole domain of meaning and value, recourse to which is indispensable for all practical reflections and decisions of policy, is disposed of as something purely "subjective," "emotional," of interest to scholars only for what it symptomizes. And teachers or students who concern themselves in depth with this side of the life of the mind are treated as pariahs who, lacking any proper objective subject-matter and methodology, therefore have no proper place in institutions of higher learning.[4]

At the Danforth workshop this past summer the effects of this ideology were everywhere apparent in the wide-spread refusal even to consider the possibility that knowledge of vital importance about the quality of life in the university has been directly revealed in the confrontations of disaffected students and their faculty allies with the authorities who preside over our scientific-technological knowledge factories. But what if these students and faculty members should really understand something not only about themselves but also about us which can only be learned in and through such confrontations? What chance have we to acquire, not to mention make use of, such knowledge when we systematically discredit its possibility? Accordingly, what can we scholars make of the contention of the single black seminar leader at the Danforth workshop, Professor Charles Long of the University of Chicago, that the sheer presence of increasing numbers of black students in our institutions of higher learning will make the meaning of "the relationship of the liberal arts to the liberation of persons and society" more intense and significant?[5]

Conflicts in the Wider Society

Such questions have their obvious analogues when we turn to the situation within the national society whose wider conflicts of power and patterns of value, or disvalue, are everywhere reflected in the academy itself. It is my own entirely unoriginal contention that virtually every important issue concerning the existing structure of the academy has its direct counterpart within the larger society.

The fact is evident in the systematic refusal of most national leaders in politics, government, and industry to take seriously the insights of oppressed minority groups and to rely rather on the presumed learning and expertise of ex- or absentee-professors who confess that they have no general theoretical knowledge of the problems they are called upon to solve. It is evident in the almost pathetic struggle on the part of young men and women, powerfully supported by their parents, to gain admission into the more prestigious university colleges and, from an early age, to confine themselves to courses of study in the secondary schools that may give them a chance of admission to such colleges. And it is evident in the very conception of "upward-bound" programs that will presumably enable "disadvantaged" students, including especially black students, to make their way through these same institutions of higher learning into remunerative positions of prestige and authority.

However, the forms of referred pain that afflict our universities have other by no means unrelated causes in the national society. One specific cause, of course, lies in our inability to conclude a futile, bloody, debilitating war in the Far East. Another lies in the devastating side effects of that war within the society, including the uncontrolled build-up of an overwhelmingly destructive military power and the increasing readiness of civil authorities to use it on the "home front" in order to preserve law and order, and the continuation of a national selective service, or draft. But the war as well as the ever more influential and extensive military establishments are themselves functions of an imperial and counter-revolutionary foreign policy which appears not only to many people in South America, Africa, and Asia, but also to our own youth and above all our black population as inherently repressive and warlike. What is worse, the latter, who not unnaturally regard this immensely costly and enervating policy as something which is maintained largely at their own expense, are thereby further alienated from the government to which they must look at the same time for economic assistance and for the protection of their existing rights.

A correlative source of the same malaise lies in the patent inability of an overwhelmingly affluent society, or else an unwillingness on the part of those who control its wealth and scientific-technological expertise, to cope effectively with any of our national disorders: the blights that afflict our cities, the waste or misuse of our national resources, the contamination of the air, water, and land, the deep pockets of corrosive poverty and misery among all "disadvantaged" peoples whether in the cities or in rural areas. These evils are not only material, but also cultural and spiritual. For they give rise to the wide-spread conviction that those who have effective control over our resources are committed in practice to maintaining their own power positions at any cost, even to themselves. In such a society, so it is argued, men no longer regard themselves as human beings but as things or artifacts to be used and manipulated simply in order to maintain the system.

39

To my mind the most distressing aspect of this situation is that the traditional aims of a government that calls itself liberal and democratic are no longer taken seriously by those who have little or no share in the determination of its policies. And the ideology of liberal democracy, with its commitment to a rule of law, now stands discredited in the eyes of the very people it is meant to benefit. Thus they become in turn advocates—and victims—of a counter-elitist ideology of separatism and sometimes of violence whose own inevitable consequence would be a form of dictatorship for which ideals of justice and legality no longer have meaning.

Unfortunately the "Others," to use Sartre's useful word, offer the people no meaningful alternative. On the contrary, their own elitist attitudes are disclosed in their fashionable but empty doctrine (derived, of all things, from Karl Marx) of the "end of ideology," which barely conceals their own counter-ideology of political "realism," hand-to-mouth pragmatism, and piecemeal social engineering. Indifferent even to existing constitutional forms and restraints, they talk endlessly about "national society" and the "national interest," of whose prevailing power structures they themselves are the primary beneficiaries.

The net result is the general sense of disillusionment and drift and of an unwillingness to take seriously the belief of idealists in our capacity as a people to make necessary radical changes in our institutional life. In more metaphysical and religious terms, one finds an increasing attenuation of the faith in man's capacity for self-action and self-transcendence.

However, these very terms are discredited by anti-ideology intellectuals who serve as apologists and front-runners for the existing establishments. As they repeatedly tell us, morality and religion themselves belong to the domain of ideology. Those who continue to speak in ethical and religious terms are thereby discredited in advance as "extremists" and "alienists" who have nothing to say to sensible men of business and affairs. Thus, systematically self-deprived of any language save the languages of science and power, do they themselves provide their opponents with formal as well as substantive justification for their own aberrant cynicism regarding the principles of our American system.

Ideology of Racism

It would be instructive at this point to chart in some detail the development of what, from an educational as well as a more general socio-political perspective, is probably the most important chapter in the story of our emerging value patterns in American society as well as the conflicts of power attending them.

Unfortunately there is space only to make the barest mention of the situation of our black population and the forms of referred pain that everywhere afflict them. Among black leaders, the idealism of Martin Luther King, which provided the main hinge of the great civil-rights movement in the fifties, is being replaced by a black-power movement whose separatism, reinforced by a mystique of despairing counter-violence, now leads black people into head-on collisions with their white adversaries. Indifferent now to belated and hypocritical appeals to principles of demo-cracy, the rule of law, and the ideal of an integrated policy of equal and free men, these leaders treat self-interested white elitists and sincere white liberals alike as a common enemy which nothing will move but determined manifestations of brute force and power. Ours, as they claim, is through and through a racist society and culture which they must combat by every means, physical and ideological, at their disposal. And the fact that they thereby become victims of a tragic ideology of black racism falls on ears now as deaf as those of their adversaries.

This ideological decline, however, can only be understood as a function of the disarray of our whole society. Until this fact is understood we will continue to misconstrue the forms of referred pain from which so many black Americans, regardless of their economic and social positions, so deeply and grievously suffer. Meanwhile, the havoc which is thereby wrought upon our entire educational system is incalculable.

However, it is not all havoc. Let us now return to the situation in our confused and revolting academy. In the preceding remarks, I have deliberately overstated the point in order to make it. Black students and teachers, like the people from which they come, are by no means merely pathetic victims of an ideology of racism and counter-violence. Like the white student-activists from whom they

41

have now unfortunately but understandably dissociated themselves, they are not only well aware of their own dignity as human beings but also of the immense value of the moral, social, and educational perspectives they have reached through long centuries of enslavement and oppression.

Black students tell us, as can no other group in America, what are the concrete meanings of such universal concepts as community, justice, and freedom, and in so doing they already help to restore our badly eroded belief in moral and, behind them, religious realities. Indeed, their very presence in the academy is a constant reminder of the primary services of the colleges and universities in a democratic society: the fitting of *all* citizens not only for forms of work which will make use of their own best intellectual energies, but also for an encompassing *human* existence in which the whole mind of man may at last fulfill itself.

Need for Political Action

But there is another more practical lesson to be learned from the ever increasing numbers of self-disciplined black insurgents on our campuses. With their various "nonnegotiable" demands, for the sake of which they are prepared to sacrifice themselves in order to tie up the daily routines of whole universities, they show the rest of the academic community many things it needs to know about its own power and the human uses to which it may be put. They show us, for example, how the power of the entire academy might be used for wider educational purposes through organized, if sometimes unconventional, activities like their own.

Who knows, if we stood together and were willing not only to form lobbies but to organize our own sit-ins or even general strikes against punitive legislators and governors, not to mention a reactionary congress and president that cares more about law and order on the campus than about the quality of the education offered there, we might well effect a new understanding of the higher learning as well as radical reconstruction of our conceptions of its services to the national society. Were we ourselves exigently to make our own nonnegotiable demands, no doubt at considerable cost to ourselves, for far larger grants-in-aid and scholarships for disadvantaged students and for better, more extensive nonelitist "upward-bound" programs for those now inadequately prepared for college, who can say that we would not bring about a regeneration of ourselves as teachers and a reinstitution of that sense of community which is so sadly missing from the contemporary university campus? It is not inconceivable that we might thereby re-establish our right to an authority and leadership as educators which our dissenting students no longer acknowledge.

One thing is clear: such possibilities, or hopes, will not be realized by scholars who simply stand and wait. We are told by conservative members of the academic establishment that the university must now be depoliticized for the sake of its perennial ends of disinterested learning and teaching. To heed such advice would be a disaster. On the contrary, just as our insurgent academy, both black and white, has taught us that significant liberal learning must concern itself with the liberation of human beings, so it has helped us see, by its own example, how academic mountains can be moved by concerted, dedicated, disciplined political action. A liberated university, in short, must liberate itself; there is no one else to do the job.

This is not to say that all the bold tactics and strategies mentioned above are practicable. Nor, certainly, is it for me to vouch for them. Like most of my kind, my knowledge extends only as far as my experience, and that experience, as I am well aware, is still far too abstract and literary. But this at least I have learned and do know: political action on the part of academicians can be a force for good as well as evil. I have also learned from my juniors in the dissenting academy that, from an educational point of view, politics can be a great "mixed good." It can serve to protect and to advance educational values, but it can also serve in the process to create them. In the domain of the higher learning, as elsewhere, men learn mainly from participating, by acting and doing. Spectatorial minds contribute nothing to the advancement of relevant human understanding.

How Late Is It?

The title of this essay is "How Late Is It?". The inescapable answer is that it is very late indeed. The power conflicts both on the campus and in the society have made it clear that, unless we

43

academicians display more care both for the protection and the enlightenment of *all* our kind, including our dissenting students and faculty, our sacred academy will not be worth saving and that its demise will not be deeply mourned by those for whom the exploration of the moon means more than the rehabilitation of the planet Earth.

Our student activists have taught us the inestimable lesson of refusal and the immense liberation that comes from refusal. It always remains within our power to say "No!" to militarists and industrialists who employ our services in defense of a national interest about whose ends we have not been consulted. And it is within our power to say "No!" to their academic lackies. Should we say it together and with conviction, I am convinced that simple "No!" would do more to revitalize the higher learning in America than a thousand grants-in-aid from the government and the foundations.

---

[1]It may be helpful to describe briefly some of the salient features of the Danforth workshop. First of all, the Danforth Foundation is one of the most thoughtful as well as liberal of the larger foundations. Its deep but non-sectarian religious orientation lends a particular seriousness to the various projects and activities which it supports.

The lay membership of the Danforth workshop changes from year to year, since no individual college or university is represented for two years running. However, the workshop mix, with minor variations, changes only slowly. Included are representatives of great state and private universities as well as of four-year colleges whose very accreditation is marginal; representatives of new urban community universities and of colleges in rural back-waters; representatives both of aggressively secular academies and poor denominational schools. There are deans and department heads, lively and often dissident junior professors and instructors. There are research scholars with connections in industry and government and overworked teachers whose duties preclude the luxury of sustained independent study. There are men whose reputations extend no farther than their campuses and others whose reputations are national.

The workshop seminar leaders are selected not only for the variety of their academic interests but also for the diversity of their educational perspectives and philosophies. Some are scientists, others psychologists and social scientists, still others, humanists and professional educationists. One or two seminar leaders hold administrative posts, but most are professors whose energies are committed mainly to teaching and research in their respective fields of inquiry. And, like the lay members of the workshop, the seminar leaders come from universities and colleges in different parts of the country.

The varied activities of the workshop include seminars, lectures, panel discussions, and many extracurricular activities, formal and informal, including many continuing discussions that go on sometimes into the later hours within the "shadow workshop," as I call it, which bears such a striking resemblance to the "shadow university."

In sum, the workshop becomes a microcosmic semiacademy. And just because our time is so short, the various points of view represented, the resultant tensions, the hopes and fears expressed, achieve an unusual compression and clarity of definition which serves the purposes of this paper extremely well.

[2]One noteworthy feature of the present hardening of attitudes within the university is a noticeable self-division within the ranks of the administrators themselves.

[3]Of course, there is nearly always an escape clause built into such demands. At

44

Brandeis, for example, the demands of revolting black students were nonnegotiable but their "meaning" was not.

[4]One distinguished excolleague of mine at Harvard, never pausing to consider the rationale of his own God-given values, simply disposes of such people as mere "attitudinizers" who perhaps may be tolerated in times of tranquility, but simply put down when they refuse to keep their place.

[5]Quoted from an unpublished typescript entitled "Impressions of the Danforth Workshop on the Liberal Arts," by Charles Long.

Precis

The public has a legitimate interest in higher education because higher education contributes to the progress and growth of society through research and the production of skilled and informed manpower. The public is particularly concerned about the cost of higher education, because the public finances higher education and is the ultimate consumer of its output.

There is a communication gap between the public and higher education. Greater dialogue between the two is needed. Higher education's goals, objectives, policies, and practices are dependent upon this dialogue, especially if the public's needs are to be served by higher education.

The public is ready to assert its interest in higher education. Communication between higher education and the public either will become a dialogue, or it will become a one-way flow from the public to higher education. The public, through its representative bodies, is becoming more involved in outlining overall educational policies, defining goals, and determining functions of higher education. I feel this trend will increase.

Public involvement resulting from basic changes in our society will mean substantial and rapid change for higher education. Higher education's inability to respond rapidly to change has caused a breach between it and the public it serves. In order to close this breach there must be greater public involvement in defining society's needs to higher education. This will require a number of changes in how we manage higher education.

The management of higher education needs to be improved to meet challenges of a new and different dimension. Higher education must be prepared to measure its products to see if its efforts are meeting the objectives set forth by the public bodies. This will require that higher education become involved with management by objectives; utilize such management techniques as planning, programming, and budgeting systems (PPBS); and develop management information systems.

The speed with which higher education institutes better management practices and the public assumes an active role in the determination of objectives will be the measure of how soon we can respond effectively to today's problems.

46

HIGHER EDUCATION:
THE PUBLIC INTEREST

Richard L. Rosenberg
President, Associated Chemists, Inc.
Chairman, Oregon State Educational Coordinating Council

Addressing oneself to the premise that social change of our society has affected the power structure of the university is in itself a step toward solution of our existing problem. We are admitting that there is a social change and that the university may very well be affected by this change.

The accurate appraisal of what social changes will cause what effects in universities throughout the U.S. is a speculative subject. We have quite a few recent occurrences from which we may draw conclusions in projecting what our future problems will be and how the various elements of our society will react to these problems.

My exposure to recent events, my beliefs formed by three years of active participation in the Oregon Educational Coordinating Council, and my 20 years in business management are the basis for the following comments. I tend to think that the following beliefs are shared in large measure by others on educational boards as well as by a large segment of the public.

Definition of "Public"

It is well to point out at this juncture what I intend the word "public" to mean in the context of these remarks. The public is defined here by exclusion rather than inclusion. In other words, I am using the term public to mean all of us, excluding only professional educators and administrators. It is meant to be inclusive of everyone else: all faiths, all colors, all economic levels, students, laborers, professional people, the man on the street or in the slum; and their voice the legislature and public boards and commissions.

Five Basic Beliefs

In approaching this subject of the public's interest in higher education, I have several basic beliefs that I would like to cover here. I believe that:

1. The public has a legitimate interest in higher education.
2. There is a communication gap between the public and higher education.
3. The public is ready to assert its interest in higher education.
4. Public involvement, resulting from basic changes in our society, will mean a substantial and rapid change for higher education.
5. Finally, management of higher education must be improved to meet the challenges of a new and different dimension.

I'm sure none of these beliefs are new to any of you, but perhaps when examining them in the light of this conference, we can gain some insights.

The Public Has a Legitimate Interest in Higher Education

I think one thing that must be understood is that the public has an interest in higher education because higher education contributes to the progress and growth of our society. Our educational institutions endeavor to prepare the professional people, managers, researchers, and artists who will provide leadership for, and participate in, an advanced technological state. Virtually every economic, social, and cultural endeavor is dependent on higher education's production of this skilled and informed manpower. Higher education also performs a substantial portion of the research required in this country—research that ranges all the way from the development of better seeds to exotic uses of nuclear energy and makes significant contributions toward a better tomorrow.

48

The public has an interest in what higher education costs. The public finances higher education. It is the ultimate consumer of the output of higher education. In this era of ever-increasing taxes, higher education is demanding a substantially greater portion of the total tax revenue. Is it any wonder that the public is interested in how higher education is utilizing its resources? Public pressure to improve the effectiveness and efficiency of these resources will increase as the competition for the tax dollar increases in the years to come. I may be oversensitive on this point because of my background as a manufacturer, but it is unlikely that the public will continue to increase its support of higher education without much more precise descriptions of higher education's objectives and an evaluation of how well these objectives are being met.

There Is a Communication Gap Between the Public and Higher Education

There is need for a greater dialogue between higher education and the public. Higher education's goals, objectives, policies, and practices are dependent upon this dialogue, especially if the public's needs are to be served by higher education.

Higher education cannot allow this communication gap to continue. Legislatures are addressing themselves to the definition of goals and guidelines for higher educational systems in their respective states. Higher education needs to inform the members of the legislature and the public at large of its problems and needs before goals and guidelines which may be opposed to the institution's best interests are imposed. If this happens because of a lack of information and understanding, created by a communication gap, higher education will have only itself to blame.

Only when higher education needs to pass a new tax base or bond issue does it demonstrate its excellent ability to communicate. Communication on other occasions is sparse or in "educationalese," which confuses rather than communicates with the public.

The public has also contributed to the communication problem. Those of us who represent the public by serving in legislatures or on boards and commissions must do a better job of articulating the public needs that can legitimately be met by higher education.

49

We now find ourselves in a situation where persons and groups are not talking to each other. As a result, ingrained prejudices are leading to biased perceptions, misrepresentations, and over-reactions. Fault lies with the public for not seeking better communication more actively, and with higher education for not fostering it.

Higher education is well equipped to create an informed public. It should consider professionally directed public relations as a necessary on-going activity. The public is actively seeking information today as never before. The time has come for higher education to explain its activities and enlist support for its concerns.

I would urge that public bodies, such as coordinating councils, boards, and commissions, take a posture of mediation rather than a position of advocacy. They must foster mutual trust and respect for both people in higher education and the legitimate interests of the public.

The Public Is Ready To Assert Its Interest in Higher Education

Communication between higher education and the public will either become a dialogue, or it will become a one-way flow from the public to higher education. The public, through its legislative assemblies, educational boards, and commissions, is becoming more involved in outlining overall educational policy, defining goals, and determining functions of higher education. I feel this trend will increase.

The public has been sufficiently aroused to realize that higher education has some serious problems. Because of the public's high degree of sensitivity about the level of taxation, it is natural for the public to look toward the major expenditure of these tax dollars.

The public's concern about problems in higher education, coupled with a shortage of tax dollars, has set a course for most state legislatures that has the ultimate goal of public involvement with educational policies, goals, and functions. Higher education

50

does not need to view these developments with alarm if it will face its responsibility for active cooperation now.

In order for the public to realize what it is buying for higher education expenditures, it must first decide what it should buy, needs to buy, and can buy. Qualification of what the output from higher educational institutions should be is probably one of the most important goals we, as a concerned public, need to clarify. To continue to ask the public to increase its commitment to higher education without identifying the product the institutions are to produce is, in my opinion, a program destined for fiscal failure.

In the past, educators have been relatively free to determine policy, goals, and functions without a great deal of input, other than money, from the public. However, this policy will not continue. The public will assert its interests in higher education. There will not only be a public input, but also a growing concern about output. The question that remains to be answered is whether higher education will choose to work with the representatives of the public or whether it will resist any further encroachments into an area that many feel is "off limits" to the public.

Public Involvement Resulting from Basic Changes in Our Society Will Mean Substantial and Rapid Change for Higher Education

We all recognize that there are conflicts over values or, at a minimum, changes in the emphasis on certain values in American society today. These changes are the by-products of an evermore complex technology, increasing urbanization, deteriorating environmental quality, breakdown of the family unit, and many other things. The net effect is that institutions of higher education must be more flexible today than ever before if they are to offer a creative response. All of us are faced with the problem of being able to react to the change in the rate of change.

Higher education's inability to respond rapidly to change has caused a breach between it and the public it serves. In order to close this breach, there must be greater public involvement in defining society's needs to higher education. I am aware that this greater involvement may be disruptive for a period of time. Educators have not been bothered by this kind of public involvement in the past, and it is unlikely that they will readily accept a more aggressive leadership posture on the part of the public. Responsible cooperation will be needed.

We are now in the position of playing "catch up" for what we failed to do in the past. I hope that neither the public nor higher education will over-react. Higher education has served the public well in the past and I would expect it to do so in the future. Modifications need to be made, and in some instances, the total approach should be changed.

If we believe in the value of education as one of the principal motivating forces for social change and improvement, then we must gear the educational system to the needs of the society. We have to recognize that we must educate students to enter a society with different needs and goals then those of the past. The needs have been thrust upon us as much as they have been established by thoughtful planning.

Some of us may not like the changes being thrust upon us, and it may be beneficial to attempt to offset some of these changes in the future, but we must deal with the present crisis now. This will require a number of changes in how we manage higher education.

Higher education needs excellence in management as never before in order to meet the challenge of the next decade.

The Management of Higher Education Needs To Be Improved To Meet Challenges of a New and Different Dimension

The public, reacting through its legislatures and its public educational boards and commissions, will expect better management of its institutions of higher education. It is unlikely that the public will continue to condone higher education managed by persons who are renowned scholars but who are untrained in modern management techniques, to allow inefficient utilization of physical plants, or to be satisfied with a curriculum which is poorly designed to meet the goals and objectives required of higher education in the years ahead.

It is the responsibility of higher education to create sufficient communication with the public to insure that the public is informed. On the other hand, the public must react by supporting higher education and helping to define needed educational services by gathering information from its various segments. It will then be up to the legislatures and educational boards and commissions to interpret public intent and set overall goals toward which higher education should direct its efforts. No longer can a policy vacuum be filled by anyone who is aggressive enough to assume the policy role.

Higher education must be prepared to implement the goals set forth, to work toward previously determined objectives. It will be necessary for higher education to become involved with management by objectives; to utilize such management techniques as planning, programming, and budgeting systems (PPBS); and to develop management information systems.

Higher education must be prepared to measure its products to see if its efforts are meeting the objectives set forth by the public bodies. If the objectives are not being met, there must be the flexibility necessary to modify higher education rapidly so that objectives can be met. In short, the emphasis must change from an institutional orientation to a product or objective orientation.

When higher education becomes oriented toward public objectives, it is likely that the functions of our institutions will change, and perhaps the institution as we know it today will also change.

With clearly defined objectives, it may be found that certain higher education functions need to be handled differently or even eliminated. An example of a current problem relating to the function of higher education is the confusion surrounding research, instruction, and administration. Most institutions of higher education, especially universities, have tried to serve too many masters. Many people involved in research, instruction, and administration are making their own value judgments as to what portion of their time to devote to each task. Our firm would go bankrupt if we followed this procedure. What I am suggesting is that our institutions may be bankrupt in their ability to serve the public by the most efficient methods available today.

Why can't instruction and research be run by separate administrations, within the same institution or within separate but contiguous institutions, still making it possible to share staff? With proper instructional objectives and clearly defined research needs, specific contractual arrangements could be made with all involved personnel.

Research would need to be geared to the economic demands and social needs of the public. A clearer definition of the need for, and the success of, our expenditure for pure or applied research would be available if it operated as a separate facility.

The instructional function of the institution would not be clouded by resources of both faculty and facility diverted to research at the expense of the student. If instruction stood alone as a separate function, it would be far easier for the public to appraise and support.

Summary

In conclusion, let me emphasize that I believe the public has awakened to its responsibilities toward higher education. Open and free flowing dialogue is needed to enable the public to assist higher education in increasing its flexibility and accepting the new challenges. The speed with which higher education institutes better management practices and the public assumes an active role in the determination of objectives will be the measure of how soon we can respond effectively to today's problems. We have benefited by the identification of our problems, and a direction for the solution of these problems is becoming clear. We now need large amounts of active listening, as well as cooperation and communication from all levels of those involved—students, faculty, administration, and the public.

Precis

Conflicts in faculty members' interests and values arise out of changing patterns of authority, power, and influence in higher education.

The intimate relationships of many universities with government, industry, and the military raise serious questions of ethical responsibility and intellectual independence for both faculty members and institutions. There is ever present danger of conflict of interest, of gross neglect of university responsibilities, and perversion of the ethical values of the academy. Because of this, the time has come for universities to require faculty members to secure formal approval of all major outside sources of research funds and all major consulting contracts.

The close relationships of individual faculty members and institutions with industry and national defense also raise important questions of individual, collective, and corporate accountability.

To whom is the faculty member accountable? He is accountable to his individual conscience, has scholarly peers, his students, and his institution. In addition, faculty members and institutions are publicly accountable in manifold ways. The trend is for universities and colleges to become instruments of public policy to an increasing degree. These forms of accountability are multiple and sometimes conflicting.

The inevitable tension between professional autonomy and accountability is heightened by internal devisiveness and conflict, not only between the faculty and the administration or the governing board, but also between faculty groups struggling for power. On many campuses an adversary spirit is rapidly replacing efforts to establish collaborative methods of government. Unions, collective bargaining, sanctions, and other aspects of professional negotiations are becoming increasingly common.

I predict that the spirit of confrontation and relationships of an adversary character will intensify in many colleges and universities during the next decade. We have moved into an era of conflict and turmoil. The way we handle controversy, conflict and turbulence will determine the future of our institutions. There is reason to doubt that the traditional appeal of reason and persuasion will resolve the discord. Is there any hope, then, of reuniting a house divided?

FACULTY INTERESTS IN
VALUE CHANGE AND POWER CONFLICT*

T.R. McConnell
Research Educator

Center for Research and Development
in Higher Education

University of California, Berkeley

Conflicts in faculty members' interests and values arise out of changing patterns of authority, power, and influence in higher education. The intimate relationships of many universities with government, industry, and the military raise serious questions of ethical responsibility and intellectual independence for both faculty members and institutions. In both their internal and external relationships, faculty members are striving for status as professionals. As such they have attained a high degree of individual and collective autonomy. But this autonomy is by no means absolute. Individuals find themselves accountable to other members of the academic community and to the institution itself. Both faculty members and their institutions are also publicly accountable in manifold ways. These forms of accountability are multiple and sometimes conflicting.

The inevitable tension between autonomy and accountability, both individual and institutional, will be heightened by internal divisiveness and conflict, not only between the faculty and the administration, or between the faculty and the governing board, but also between faculty groups struggling for power. There is reason to doubt that the traditional appeal to reason and persuasion will resolve the discord. Is there any hope, then, of reuniting a house divided?

*This paper was prepared with the assistance of Mr. Ronald Farland.

These are the problems and questions which are discussed below.

The Military-Industrial-University Complex

In 1968 the federal government spent $4.7 billion on higher education. The great beneficiaries of this bounty, according to a recent analysis by Clark Kerr, were the faculties, first in agriculture, then in atomic physics, medicine, and space science. The individual faculty member profited enormously from federal subventions. As Kerr put it:

> He was happily faced by a seller's market. He had a second source of funds in the agency in Washington. He became more mobile . . . teaching loads went down, salaries went up, facilities improved. Faculty members became more like independent contractors. . . . The sum of 1.5 billion dollars a year for research, mostly to individual faculty members, has changed the relation of faculty members to the institutions of higher education. The Federal government bought research, and individual faculty members took the money and bought their independence.[1]

Military Research and University Values

It is not surprising that the values of these "independent contractors" have become the values of the market place or the governmental arena. Neither is it particularly surprising that many faculty members have become deeply involved in research projects which are inimical to the openness which presumably characterizes the academic community. Some institutions, for example, have become implicated in classified war-related research. Concealment is inconsistent with the free exchange, criticism, and dissemination of ideas. It is this free market in ideas which generates the vitality and protects the integrity of the university. Many students, and an increasing number of faculty members, believe that by engaging in secret, military research, the university has corrupted its moral values and perverted its intellectual purposes. Years ago, as a university administrator, I opposed the acceptance of classified projects, and I still believe that faculties, administrators, and governing boards should renounce secret research as incompatible with the ideals of the university.

After World War II, the British segregated classified research in government laboratories. Although the universities realized that these establishments would compete for scientists and research funds, they nevertheless decided that this was not too high a price to pay for protecting their intellectual freedom. As time has gone on, university and government research laboratories have developed mutually beneficial relationships. But the policy of segregating classified investigation and military research has been maintained.

I should like to see the universities in the United States withdraw from the defense research establishments which some of them jointly or singly administer. I should be very much happier if the University of California ceased to administer the Livermore Laboratory, or any other agency engaged in research on weaponry or other forms of warfare. I was encouraged when some 80 Berkeley faculty members and graduate students recently pledged not to engage in war research or weapons production. (The UCLA faculty, however, voted 514 to 329 *against* the proposition that the Los Alamos and Livermore weapons development and testing centers be separated from the university.)

Relations of University and Industry

We not only have a university-military complex on our hands. We also have a university-industrial combine which is even more pervasive and which has been far more powerful in determining the shape of the university and in engaging the loyalties of its faculties. The universities have supplied the scientific, technological, and managerial manpower for the industrial society. Likewise, they are now providing the science and technology which the techno-structure requires.

Industry has contributed vast sums to universities to accelerate the flow of knowledge on which technological advancement depends. This infusion of research support assures access by great industries and corporations to university scientists and scholars. Galbraith has observed that so intimate is the connection between education and industry that the business executive no longer accepts membership on a university board of trustees as a position of social prestige, or as a strategic place to curb radical social ideas.

His trusteeship, according to Galbraith, gives him an opportunity to keep in touch with sources of specialized talent, scientific discoveries, and technological innovations. This is essential to the corporation because ". . . the modern scholar of science, mathematics, information systems or communications theory is ever more in demand to guide the mature corporation through its besetting problems of science, technology and computerization."[2]

Conflicts of Interest

The conflict of interest that may emerge from the close association of the university with industry was recently illustrated when it was revealed that the National Forests Products Association had paid the expenses of the dean of the School of Forestry at Berkeley to testify before a congressional committee investigating a proposal to increase cutting in the national forests. At about the same time, a California state official charged on television that some faculty members in the University of California had declined to testify at an investigation of oil well leakage in the Santa Barbara Channel. (Others later agreed to testify.) The same official asserted that certain heads of departments of petroleum engineering in the university frankly admitted that they couldn't afford to testify because their departments were dependent on the petroleum industry for research funds.

It is this kind of apparent conflict of interest and questionable influence that leads students to condemn universities as the tools of special interests and the pawns of the economic establishment.

Because they possess the specialized knowledge which modern government and industry require, many faculty members have developed a lucrative consulting practice. This was once mainly confined to scientists and engineers but is now common in many professional schools, including business administration, education, criminology, law, and so on. Professors of economics, industrial relations, psychology, and even sociology have saleable expertise. Humanists are about the only faculty left without lucrative businesses; they have to be content with occasional poetry readings, lectures, or appearances as critics on television. This may be one reason why so many modern faculty dissidents are found in the English department.

60

Many faculty entrepreneurs make as much from consulting fees as from their university appointments. Consequently, as Galbraith has pointed out, not only are· they likely to identify themselves with the goals and values of the enterprises they serve, but also they are likely to spend more time on airplanes than in their offices. To this, graduate students will angrily testify.

Because of the ever present danger of conflict of interest, of gross neglect of university responsibilities and perversion of the ethical values of the academy, the time has come for universities to require faculty members to secure formal approval of all major outside sources of research funds and all major consulting contracts. Faculty members should be required to make full disclosure of income from such external sources and of the extent to which outside activities interfere with normal university obligations. Disclosure in itself will not assure the supremacy of the values of the academy over the values of the market place. That supremacy will come, as Galbraith has said, only when the university asserts its control over the education it provides and the research it conducts, exercises its options for skepticism and criticism, and honors the primacy of intellectual and esthetic over materialistic values.

Autonomy and Accountability

The intimate relationships of individual faculty members and institutions with industry and national defense raise important questions of individual, collective, and corporate accountability. I use the term "accountability" in the ordinary dictionary sense of being answerable for one's conduct. Accountability and autonomy are interdependent. An individual loses autonomy to the extent to which he is answerable to an external agent. Likewise, a university faculty cannot be completely autonomous if it is accountable to an administrative officer or to a board of trustees. The corporate university is not completely independent if it is answerable to donors, the legislature, or the electorate. Let us turn first to individual accountability. To whom is a faculty member accountable?

Accountability to Personal Standards

First of all, perhaps, a faculty member is accountable to his own conscience, and especially to his own standards of scholarship and intellectual integrity. The "Statement on Professional Ethics" of the AAUP points out that the faculty member's "primary responsibility to his subject is to seek and to state the truth as he sees it .... He accepts the obligation to exercise critical self-discipline and judgment in using, extending, and transmitting knowledge. He practices intellectual honesty." Presumably these are internalized values and deep-seated ethical commitments.

Most of us are willing to accommodate differences or to adjust to some circumstances. But most of us also have some principles we will not violate, some point beyond which we will not compromise. Thus, we hold ourselves accountable to our own ideals.

Accountability to Peers

As professionals, we are also answerable to our scholarly peers. Sometimes the faculty member is accountable only informally, as when other scholars appraise his research. Sometimes the accountability is formal, as is the case when a faculty committee evaluates the individual's performance as a basis for appointment, promotion, tenure, or discontinuance.

A recent example of informal evaluation of research and scholarship by a faculty member's peers occurred at Berkeley. In a now famous paper in the *Harvard Educational Review*[3], Professor Arthur Jensen of the School of Education analyzed racial differences in intelligence between black and white children. He concluded that heritability is a much more influential factor than environment in determining mental capacity. This is one of the reasons, he said, why compensatory educational programs have met almost uniformly with failure.

Subsequently the local chapter of SDS denounced Professor Jensen as a racist, and in letters to the *Daily Californian* various persons demanded his dismissal.

However, a group of scholars wrote to the *Daily*, stating that:

... nobody has shown that Arthur Jensen's research is dishonest or that his data have been deliberately distorted. . . . We could demonstrate that he has been extremely naive about the nature of cultural differences in test performances, and we find he has made erroneous assumptions about children's verbal skills, so we disagree strongly with many inferences he has made from his studies, and we are therefore appalled that educational policies might be based on them.[4]

Later Professor Jensen participated in a symposium on "Genetic and Environmental Determinants of Intelligence," in which scholars from genetics, sociology, education, and psychology criticized his research findings and interpretations. The outcome of this debate is not important here. The symposium's significance is that it was a concrete instance of the way in which qualified scholars may hold another academic man accountable for the rigorousness of his research and the validity of his conclusions.

Scholars are also accountable to the great body of their colleagues, since the acts of a few may endanger the intellectual freedom of all. "As a colleague," said the AAUP, "the professor has obligations that derive from common membership in the community of scholars. He respects and defends the free inquiry of his associates." On some campuses torn by violent student disruption, faculties have wavered in their commitment to freedom of teaching, freedom of learning, and freedom of expression on all sides of a disputed issue. They have tolerated disruption of classes, intimidation of professors, and suppression of dissenting voices. Faculty members who fail to support the full freedom of the academy fail their own colleagues. *Faculty members are accountable to one another for keeping the university intellectually free.*

Accountability to Students

Faculty members are accountable to their students in a variety of ways. Presumably, they are accountable for the effectiveness of their teaching. Here and there students have evaluated their teachers, often with questionable validity and reliability. In the future, student evaluation will become more common, more systematic, and it will have more effect on faculty retention and advancement. Teachers will become accountable to students for permitting freedom of expression, including the right to differ

63

with their teachers' views. Students will be protected against prejudiced or capricious academic evaluation. Professors will be accountable to students for confidentiality concerning the latters' beliefs and political associations.[5]

Many faculty members have been insistent on their own academic freedom but have been careless about the academic freedom of students. Too frequently, college teachers have circumscribed the right to question, criticize, and dissent in the classroom. Faculty members who violate the intellectual freedom of the classroom will not go unscathed when students, as I am sure they ultimately will, turn against those teachers who, consciously or unconsciously, attempt to induce intellectual conformity. And if a recent attempt to distinguish the rights and responsibilities of faculty members from the rights and responsibilities of students is any indication, the students have a cause.

Dr. Charles Frankel, professor of philosophy at Columbia University, recently declared the classroom out of bounds so far as students' assertion of *lernfreiheit* is concerned. He asserted that no college or university has an obligation to present all ideas or all points of view in the name of academic freedom. He wrote:

> The ideas or opinions represented in the collegiate program of education must be simply the ideas and points of view presented by persons who, in the judgment of their colleagues, are competent practitioners of their disciplines. The right of any opinion to be heard, which is a right outside the campus, does not apply to the classroom. And this is not because the college does not practice free inquiry. It is because free scholarly inquiry is inquiry controlled and governed by scholars in accordance with their own standards.[6]

According to Frankel, the students' right to present their points of view, to bring in spokesmen for their ideas, or to examine alternatives to their teachers' views, will have to be exercised outside the classroom. This, according to Frankel, is the nature and extent of students' academic freedom.

To my mind, this is an archaic and indefensible position, and it is not one which intellectually curious and independent students will accept. Frankel's attitude is certainly contrary to the classic treatment of academic freedom by MacIver, who wrote that in any educational system " . . . the breath of life dies within it unless the student is freely permitted, indeed encouraged, to think for himself, to question, to discuss, and to differ."[7] He went on to say that:

> . . . an educator who does not reasonably present the pros and cons of a highly debatable issue, who does not first examine both with decent care, who treats unverified hypotheses as though they were invincible verities, is betraying his discipline and rejecting the primary ground on which he is entitled to professional status or respect.[8]

This is exactly the test of *lernfreiheit* which able and alert students will apply to their teachers.

Let me add that MacIver, I feel sure, would not have condoned efforts by students to supplant their teachers' ideas with their own dogmas, or to suppress the ideas of either faculty or students who dissent from the students' own special orthodoxies. For students, even intellectually able ones, do have such orthodoxies.

In a sense, what I have just been talking about is accountability to students for the content and methods of teaching. But there are other aspects of accountability which the teacher must respect at the same time, such as accountability to the canons of scholarship, intellectual integrity, and fundamental educational values. Students are justified in insisting that what they study should be germane to the interests, values, and issues which engage them personally and which define the problems of their own time. There is nothing new about this. To make education both personally and socially meaningful was the purpose of the general education movement which flowered a generation ago. It was then that Sidney Hook wrote:

> To what in the present should the content of study be relevant? In the broadest sense of the term, to the fundamental problems of the age—to the social, political, intellectual and, if we like, the spiritual questions posed by our time and culture.[9]

Hook went on to say that this was no cult of immediacy. The study of contemporary issues should not ignore the historical background which gives meaning to present events. After all, primitive man had little vision of the future because he had little sense of the past. There is no point in making modern education equally parochial.

Neither would we be justified in encouraging students to think that the problems of their society are capable of simple solution. Field trips, immersion in the life of the ghetto, spasmodic protests against the war and the draft may be lively and useful background for serious studies of racism and war. But by now it should be obvious to the most socially concerned students that the problems of racial equality and peace are extremely complicated.

To devise means of overcoming educational and cultural deprivation and of extending social and economic equality to blacks and other minorities will challenge the scholarship of educators, economists, sociologists, psychologists, and anthropologists. This is a case in which social action must be informed and guided by intellectual analysis. Faculty members' accountability to students is not merely to their immediate concerns; it is likewise accountability to the necessity for intellectualizing problems without dehumanizing them or blunting their urgency.

Accountability to the Institution

Finally, there must be some fundamental sense in which faculty members are accountable to their institution.

One of their major responsibilities is to lend every effort to the maintenance of sufficient stability in the institution to enable it to carry on its teaching, research, and service in an atmosphere of intellectual freedom, and freedom from coercion and intimidation. surely not many faculty members believe that universities can survive recurrent violence, or even recurrent disruption of teaching, learning and investigation, any more than a true university can survive without self-criticism and controversy.

It is increasingly apparent that student rebelliousness cannot be contained within tolerable grounds unless the main body of the faculty and the administrative officers—and students—can agree on a constructive policy of university life, the conditions for

66

continuing renewal, the means of maintaining stability during change, and the penalties for serious infraction of the standards and operative rules of the community. Yet this concordance has often been wanting. Administrators have often been derelict in their responsibility to consult students and faculty members, to promote reform in education and internal governance, and to plan means of appropriate response to disruption of the academic community.

Faculties have been chronically and notoriously laggard in adapting undergraduate education to the interests of new generations of students. Student protests against irrelevance have hardly sparked an educational revolution. A recent study of faculty attitudes toward student participation in governance and academic policy conducted at the Center for Research and Development in Higher Education lends little support for a strong student voice in teaching and curriculum development. Two-thirds of faculty respondents in six diverse colleges and universities were willing to give students formal responsibility for formulating social regulations, but participation in academic policy was another matter. Although 60 percent would give students some voice in the latter, only 36 percent would allow them to vote on educational policy, and but 9 percent would give students an equal vote with the faculty.[10]

Administrators have found faculties to be uncertain reeds on which to rely for support when extreme student activists or radical nonstudents interfere forcibly with the normal processes of teaching and learning. In no small number of instances, faculties have failed to support responsible administrative action or hold riotous students to account for the damage they have inflicted. Faculties are wont to urge amnesty for students who have flouted university regulations or civil law. No one would like to inflict harsh punishment for minor infractions. But everything I have learned about psychotherapy and the psychology of learning tells me that if we reward destructive behavior, we will encourage its repetition.

If faculties are irresponsible—as I think they often are—in crises precipitated by students, what are the reasons for this attitude? Some of the causes, with varying emphasis and in different combinations, are as follows:

First, faculty members are often motivated by sentiment which not infrequently verges on sentimentalism. Sentiment leads to generous, sympathetic, and impunitive regard for others—a human, humane, sensitive, and empathic reaction. Sentimentalism is an excessive emotional response which often inhibits careful discernment of motives and perception of events, especially when issues become obscure or tangled, as they usually do when the parties to a dispute resort to coercion or violence.

Second, faculties are prone to a doctrinal anti-administrative attitude. This disposition, which seems to me to have become much more widespread and deep-seated, leads faculty members to support students against "the administration." Sometimes discord between faculty and administration may be due to clear-cut philosophical differences or disagreement about practical methods for handling disputes. But frequently, the faculty's anti-administrative attitude is a doctrinaire position, based on an assumption of an irreconcilable difference in values.

Another reason for irresponsible faculty reaction is the conscious or unconscious guilt which we all share for the social ills which beset us. Our generation deserves the ignominy which youth heaps upon us. Consequently, when students attack the injustices of our society our instinct is to support them regardless of the methods they use.

We are also motivated by unconscious guilt for having failed in our responsibilities to students. Consequently, we fear that students will finally turn on us. By allying ourselves with them against administrators and other symbols of authority, we hope that students will vent their antagonism on others. I predicted several years ago that ultimately the students would turn against the faculty. This has not materialized to any great extent as yet, partly because students need allies against boards of trustees, presidents, deans, and civil authorities, and are careful not to alienate us sufficiently to lose our connivance and support.

But we will not escape forever. If they do not already know it, students will learn that it is the faculty they should hold accountable for educational reform, not the president, for it is the faculty that primarily controls the academic affairs of the institution. I still say it is only a matter of time until the student activists begin to whip the right devils.

Finally, faculties have always been fickle with respect to responsibility for student discipline. In periods of crisis, they may step in to assert control over student behavior. Once crises pass, however, they usually tire of this responsibility and turn it over again to administrative officers, usually with some remnant of faculty participation through a disciplinary committee. A more recent way for the faculty to shirk responsibility is to let external agencies control the campus.

Some institutions which have been plagued with student disorders have turned over to civil authorities all but the regulation of purely academic affairs. This was, in effect, what the Berkeley faculty did in its famous resolutions of December 8, 1964, which brought an end to the crisis precipitated by the so-called Free Speech Movement. In these resolutions, the faculty surrendered the privilege of institutional self-regulation to the external authority of the police and the courts. The resolutions provided, in essence, that the *only* control by the university over on-campus speech and political advocacy would be regulations concerning "time, place, and manner." Few other university controls over students' campus behavior still exist.

The Berkeley faculty, and the faculties of other institutions in which the civil authorities have intervened, failed to anticipate the ultimate consequences of their abdication. For a long time college and university campuses were sanctuaries of a sort, where, by unspoken consent, civil authorities let the institutions take care of all but the most serious infractions of law by students and faculty members. That sanctuary has now been lost. Not only do police departments intervene, but in some instances, at any rate, they do so without consultation with administrative officers. For example, police have raided student residences on state university campuses in New York without prior notification, much less consultation with university authorities.

Perhaps the escalation of student conflict would have made the use of police, either on their own initiative or at the call of the institution, inevitable in any case. But colleges and universities in this country will never again be relatively independent enclaves permitted to monitor most of their members' behavior. More than ever before, they are subject to the environment around them. The ivy walls come tumbling down as the waves of student protest and civil reaction flow back and forth across campus boundaries.

The overt forces playing on the academic community are but the outward manifestations of subtle changes in character and spirit, as well as in authority, power, and influence, which have inescapably altered the life and spirit of collegiate institutions.

Fortunately, colleges and universities are no longer ivory towers. They have a responsibility to criticize the world around them when it needs criticism, and to propose ways of remaking it. While it is of the world, the university must also be different from the world if it is to point the way to a better life. Its standards of taste should be more sensitive and rewarding than those to which men ordinarily hold. Its values should be more humane, more enriching of inner life, more refining of human relationships, than those of the market place. Its purposes should be nobler than the struggle for power, for superiority, or for domination over others.

Sir Douglas Logan, the principal of the University of London, wrote in his last annual report that ". . . any community, if it is to survive, must have accepted rules of conduct over and above those which can be legally enforced."[11] There are some who still believe that the noblest ideals of the university community will not survive if its canons of decency, humanity, and justice are the minimum standards of the society at large.

Professional Autonomy

I have talked about the accountability of the faculty to their individual consciences, their scholarly peers, their students, and their institution. In addition, as the group which carries major responsibility for the educational quality and program of the institution, the faculty has a broad social, and therefore general public, accountability. This is the element of accountability that the academic man is most loath to acknowledge. One reason for this is that he has a strong tradition of individual and scholarly autonomy. For a long time he has been striving for the status of an

70

independent professional. In the meantime, however, some of the oldest professions have found themselves increasingly answerable to society for professional service.

The ideal professional is still the independent practitioner associated with other specialists in a voluntary organization designed to protect him and to safeguard the public interest. Although private practice is still the norm, an increasing number of professionals are employees in large organizations such as government agencies, corporations, universities, and hospitals.

Employed professionals find it much more difficult than independent practitioners to control the conditions under which they work. Therefore, they have developed indirect sanctions to regulate their relationships with employers and are beginning to move toward the use of direct methods, such as the strike, of asserting their professional prerogatives. Nurses' associations in the Bay area have successfully used the strike to gain a dramatic improvement in salaries and working conditions. This may be a harbinger of direct action by other employed professionals, including college and university faculties. More about this later.

Garbarino has referred to the "ideal academic model" as a special example of employed professional groups. Either by formal delegation or tacit approval, college and university faculties have attained a high degree of professional self-government. They control the education and certification of entrants to the profession; the selection, retention, and promotion of their members; the content of the curriculum; work schedules; and the evaluation of performance. The individual faculty member's independence is enhanced by the principles of academic freedom and tenure. He has attained a substantial degree of personal autonomy.[12]

It should be noted, however, that even some of the old and highly autonomous professions are being subjected to social regulation. This is certainly true in the case of medicine. Physicians have been severely criticized for escalating their fees since the advent of Medicare. The administrators of Medi-Cal have revealed that some practitioners have attained enormous incomes as beneficiaries of the public systems of health care that most medical associations bitterly opposed.

71

Consequently, control over physicians' fees is inevitable. If the profession itself does not exercise reasonable control, governmental agencies will do so. As I was writing this paper, the Department of Health, Education, and Welfare established a fee schedule for Medicaid. Ultimately, I predict, the control over fees and services will be extended from the recipients of public assistance to other clients.

Medicare and Medicaid are responses to the failure of the profession to make its services available to all who need them. Unless the profession takes the initiative and responsibility for extending adequate medical care to the disadvantaged and underprivileged, society will assure such care and, if necessary, will draft professionals for this service. Ultimately, too, other health-related professions and industries will be brought under social regulation. There is obviously a clear trend toward greater social accountability on the part of individual professionals and professional associations.

Public Accountability

In many ways, college and university faculty members have been as insensitive to their clients—the students—as physicians have to theirs. Like other professionals, college teachers have an underdeveloped sense of social responsibility. If you asked faculty members, even in tax-supported institutions, whether they considered themselves publicly accountable, many of them would reply, "Certainly not." Let us look at the matter of public accountability more specifically.

It is usually said that the faculty controls courses and determines admission standards. However, it is not completely autonomous in these respects. For example, it can scarcely organize a professional curriculum without some deference to the profession itself. Again, in the long run, the citizens of a state will exert a strong influence on the selectivity of public institutions. The University of California would not find it possible to limit its admissions to students in the highest eighth of their high school classes if other institutions, specifically the state colleges and the community colleges, were not open to a much wider range of ability and achievement.

72

Any public institution, broadly speaking, takes the shape of the functions and services which various interests and various groups expect it to perform. Some of these groups are more articulate and influential than others. The University of California has long responded with alacrity to the needs of agricultural producers. Only within the last year or two has the institution shown any interest in the farm workers displaced by machines designed by its agricultural engineers.

The public university has responded primarily to the articulate, the influential, and the powerful in the citizenry, but that it has been socially responsive no one could deny. That it now must become responsive to a wider range of economic interests, as well as to a more diverse pattern of ethnic and cultural backgrounds and aspirations, no one can ignore.

Whether faculty members like it or not, they will find themselves ultimately accountable to all these publics and to the people at large.

Public Accountability Mediated

Public control over institutions of higher education is more often indirect than direct. There are several layers of representation between the people and their institutions. The people's representatives in the legislature hold the power of the purse. Governors and their executive staffs exert varying degrees of control, especially but not exclusively financial, over public institutions. Boards of trustees have the peculiar responsibility of sensitizing their institutions to the people's needs and desires, while at the same time protecting them from political interference, attacks on intellectual freedom, and misuse by special interests or powerful adversaries.

It is generally believed that governing boards can perform these functions most responsibly if they are ultimately accountable but not directly answerable to the electorate. In some states, Illinois for example, university regents are elected by the voters. The usual and preferable practice is for the governor to appoint members of the governing board for relatively long terms.

Unfortunately, in California the ex officio membership of the Governor, the Lieutenant Governor, and the Speaker of the Assembly on the Board of Regents opens the board to political interference. Critics have charged that the regents of the University of California have sometimes served as a conduit for political intervention rather than a buffer against it. Furthermore, the Berkeley Academic Senate Policy Committee has declared that, instead of protecting the university against the whims of the public mind, the regents' actions now "may be decided by the latest results of the latest poll of public opinion."

Colleges and universities not only serve the communities, the states, or the regions in which they are located. Public and private universities together also serve the national interest. Clark Kerr wrote:

> The role of higher education becomes ever more crucial to growth, as it does for the achievement of equality of opportunity, improved health care, and the general political and cultural welfare of the nation. Higher education, as Woodrow Wilson once said of Princeton, is in the "nation's service."

> The corollary of being in the service of the nation is that the nation has wishes about how it should be served. From religion to science, from agriculture to health, from depression to interplanetary probes, the nation has made its wishes known and higher education has obliged.[13]

As it expands its financial support, the nation, like the state, will hold institutions responsible for applying public funds to the purposes for which they were requested or received and, in the long run, accountable for the efficiency with which the money is used.

British University Accountability

The British universities have a very strong tradition of autonomy. But they, too, are in the public service and so they have become increasingly responsible for serving national goals, manpower needs, and educational priorities. Their public responsibility—and vulnerability—have been intensified as they have become increasingly dependent on the state for financial support.

The government is exercising increasing surveillance over the way in which universities are using public funds. As a result, they have become more and more fearful of losing their independence and of being subjected to much greater governmental intervention.

Such intervention has grown steadily, although the University Grants Committee, which is the intermediary between the government and the universities, has screened much of it from the public view. Under pressure from the Department of Education and Science, the UGC is becoming more directive. Traditionally, the committee, once it received its state appropriation, made "block" grants to the universities (supplemented by a limited number of "earmarked" allocations) which they were permitted to distribute internally as they chose. But the committee is becoming much more explicit about the purposes for which the grants are to be used.

In 1967, for the first time, the UGC, in making its grants to the institutions, sent each a letter of intent, stating the bases on which the committee had computed its allocations. It also stated the sums which it had had in mind for strengthening instruction in social studies, physics, chemistry, earth sciences, mathematics, engineering, and biological sciences. It noted the items in the university's request for which the committee had made no provision.

Presumably the UGC does not demand that the universities follow the specifications in the letter of intent. No one has any very clear idea of what retribution might follow if an institution failed to do so. To date, so far as I know, no institution has decided to make a major challenge of the UGC's and the government's authority.

The British universities have suffered a still greater incursion into their affairs by the government. Until very recently, the accounts of the universities have been open to the University Grants Committee, but not to Parliament. Now, however, the Public Accounts Committee of Parliament and the Comptroller and Auditor General have begun to inspect the universities' accounts. The Comptroller has assured the UGC and the universities that he and his staff will not raise questions concerning educational policy. It is difficult to see, of course, how it will be possible to appraise the effectiveness of financial administration without considering the purposes for which funds were expended. It seems almost inevitable that academic policy will come under Parliamentary committee review.

Since universities in the United States are used to postaudits, they would not particularly fear the financial review to which the British institutions are now being subjected. But in Britain, the inspection of university accounts presages a period of much more direct and detailed accountability to the state. Michael Beloff said recently that universities:

> ... whether academics like it or not, have become community projects. They are financed overwhelmingly by public money. Their growth, even their creation, has been dictated by social pressures and not the demands of scholastic independence. And therefore the time has come to acknowledge that internal debate alone cannot settle the priority of a university's function.[14]

The trend here and in Britain, then, is for universities and colleges to become instruments of public policy in even greater degree. The tension between institutional autonomy and public purpose and accountability will grow in intensity. It is still to be determined whether colleges and universities can serve the broader public interest and still preserve the integrity, initiative, and intellectual independence which are essential both to the free university and the free society.

A House Divided

There is little hope of maintaining intellectual freedom and integrity if our institutions are torn by divisiveness, conflict, and coercive struggles for power. Unfortunately, the prospect is for an era of confrontation and turmoil because we are a house divided. On many campuses an adversary spirit among the elements of what we once called an academic community is rapidly replacing efforts to establish collaborative methods of governance.

Factional Struggles for Power

I recently served as a member of a team studying problems of internal governance at a large, complex, public institution.[15] Its faculty is riven by two opposing factions. These groups are polarized around such issues as faculty versus administrative authority, decentralized control versus central initiative and review, and exclusive jurisdiction versus shared participation in decision-making. These are fundamental problems of governance which deserve thoughtful analysis and debate. But the factional division is hardening, and the votes on any controversial issue probably could be predicted fairly well in advance. One gets the impression that significant questions of policy are often obscured in what has become a struggle for power between the two parties. At times the struggle seems to have become a contest over power itself, rather than a dialogue over the goals of the institution or the order of priority of the purposes to be served.

The faculty has become highly politicized. In the Academic Senate and open meetings of senate committees, methods of influence used are not only the ordinary political ones like caucusing and getting out the votes, but include on occasion such devices as organizing pressure groups to attend open committee sessions. A small number of persons on both sides have become so personally and emotionally involved that they resort to invective. Attempts at a consensus, for the most part, have been abandoned. The dominant faction has excluded members of the other "party" from membership on the powerful Executive Committee of the Senate. Other committees, with one possible exception, are loaded with members of the faction in power.

Although the president of the institution has final formal authority (except that reserved to the system of which the college is a part) over academic policy and personnel, the Constitution of the Academic Assembly of the College provides that ". . . the faculty body should have responsibility and authority to develop and recommend policies and should be consulted on all academic policy matters by the president of the College." Furthermore, the approved consultative procedures regulating faculty-administrative relationships provide that "the ultimate purpose of consultative procedures shall be to guarantee full participation by faculty and academic administrators in the formulation of policies and procedures affecting the administrative and academic environment."

In spite of this principle of joint participation in decision-making, some faculty members take the position that providing information to administrative officers satisfies the requirement of consultation. A small minority of the faculty insists that consultation should take place only at the end and at the top, e.g., when a fully developed proposal or recommendation is placed before the administrative officer for approval or disapproval. This attitude is indicative of a spirit of confrontation. It is the attitude which led an observer of the academic scene to say recently:

> We seem destined . . . to move increasingly toward relationships of an adversary type, characterized by confrontation and bargaining, backed by force, by threat, and intimidation.[16]

Faculty Associations Divisive

On the campus I have been discussing, five professional associations are vying for membership and influence. The relationships of these organizations to the two major faculty factions are by no means clear-cut, but they certainly accentuate rather than attenuate the divisiveness in the faculty. The differences in philosophy and methods between the American Association of University Professors, the American Federation of Teachers, and, in California, the Association of California State College Professors make it almost impossible, in some highly polarized institutions, to develop a constructive program of educational and administrative reform that is essential to the restoration of stability on campuses plagued by disruption and rebellion.

One of the sad aspects of the recent near disintegration of San Francisco State College was the apparent inability of a large body of the faculty to agree on a program for reconstruction. An institution which cannot mobilize the faculty will and voice is sick indeed. The National Commission on the Causes and the Prevention of Violence put the matter pointedly when it said:

> (The university) can prevail only when the great majority of its members share its commitment to rational discourse, listen closely to those with conflicting views, and stand together against the few who would impose their will on everyone else.

The fundamental, and in many ways decisive, division between professional organizations is that which distinguishes the American Association of University Professors from the American Federation of Teachers. Crudely put, the division is between the principle of shared decision-making and shared authority in a community with common interests, on the one hand; and on the other, the assumption of permanent conflict of interest between faculty and administration, requiring confrontation, collective bargaining, and coercive sanctions.

The AAUP's principle of shared authority and responsibility has been defined as follows:

> . . . among the faculty, the administration, and the governing board there is an inescapable interdependence and . . . these three components have joint authority and responsibility for governing the institution . . . . The essential and overriding idea is that the enterprise is joint and that there must be adequate communication among these components, and full opportunity for appropriate joint planning and effort.[17]

The policy of the American Federation of Teachers, on the other hand, is to confront power with power. Using the industrial analogy, Dr. Israel Kugler, President of the United Federation of College Teachers, AFL-CIO, put the position as follows:

> The board of directors is the board of trustees; the managers are the presidents and the host of deans. It is these groups that wield the power and authority and determine the destiny of a university. To be sure, they have woven a web of faculty senates and councils which simulate the original role of policy-making that university faculties once had. The advisory nature of these bodies provides them with some active role in curriculum and student affairs, but virtually no part to play in securing the necessary finances to provide professional salaries, work load, and working conditions.[18]

The AFT believes that as employed professionals, college teachers should resort to collective bargaining, and if necessary, the strike. Said Kugler:

> Collective bargaining provides negotiations under conditions of equality between the trustees-administrators and the teaching staff. The cant and hypocrisy of all sorts of advisory

intramural faculty committees, senates, and councils are swept away and real negotiations can take place.[19]

Collective Bargaining and the Strike

After pointing out that his commitment to research and teaching provides the moral legitimacy for the professor's claim to professional autonomy, Kadish contended that collective bargaining and the strike are incompatible with the teacher's professional ideals. He wrote:

> What is involved in the regularized use of the strike in a collective bargaining relationship . . . is shifting the basis of professorial claims from common commitment and moral entitlement to the play of power in a competitive context. The move from academic senate to collective bargaining backed by the strike is a move to the market place, and the spirit of the market place is that you are entitled to what you can exact, and what you can exact is what you are entitled to.[20]

Kadish also asserted that the strike endangers the system of governance which he believes holds the greatest promise for effective progress in research and education. "I have in mind," he said, "the potential destructiveness of the collective bargaining strike to cooperative and shared decision-making between the faculty and the administration and the governing board of the university."

In spite of its opposition to the strike, the AAUP, under competitive pressure from the AFT and other professional organizations, has retreated from its earlier absolute position. It now says that although the strike is:

> . . . inappropriate as a mechanism for the resolution of most conflicts within higher education,

nevertheless:

> . . . situations may arise affecting a college or university which so flagrantly violate academic freedom (of students as well as of faculty) or the principles of academic government, and which are so resistant to rational methods of discussion, persuasion, and conciliation, that faculty members may feel

impelled to express their condemnation by withholding their services, either individually or in concert with others.[21]

And at the end of his article, Kadish came around to the modified AAUP position.[22]

Whatever one's view of unionism, collective bargaining, and the strike, he is forced to conclude, I believe, that collective bargaining will become much more common than it is today. Garbarino forecast that:

> ... organizations of professional employees—both those which call themselves unions and those which do not—will increasingly take their ideology and their rhetoric from the general employed professional model, their goals and status aspirations from the academic model, and their tactics from the union model. In brief, they will do their best to look and sound like professional societies, but, if necessary, will act more like unions.[23]

Several states have enacted laws giving public employees, including faculties of colleges and universities, the right to select a bargaining representative and to engage in collective bargaining. (Some of the states specifically deny public employees the right to strike.) The American Council on Education recently reported a survey which showed that 80 percent of the council's institutional members, 81 percent of other council members, and 75 percent of faculty members queried thought that there is an even chance or better that collective bargaining will be widely adopted as a method of determining faculty salaries and conditions of employment. However, 91 percent, 73 percent, and 56 percent of the respective groups considered collective bargaining to be undesirable or detrimental.[24]

It has been said that governing boards and administrations probably will get the kind of professional relations and organizations they deserve. It is significant that the greatest growth of unionism and collective bargaining seems to be taking place in junior colleges and multipurpose public colleges and universities which, as former teachers colleges, have had a tradition of administrative domination and niggardly faculty participation. Unionism will also develop rapidly in institutions whose governing boards chronically interfere with the normal processes of internal governance, especially faculty control over its own membership and over the curriculum. It was said, for example, that the membership of the AFT local at Berkeley soared after the Board of Regents withdrew the authority it had previously delegated to the campuses to appoint and promote members of the faculty.

A House Reunited?

This is obviously not a careful analysis of faculty associations, unions, collective bargaining, sanctions, and other aspects of professional negotiations in higher education. My purpose at the moment is to predict that the spirit of confrontation and relationships of an adversary character will intensify in many colleges and universities during the next decade. We have moved into an era of conflict and turmoil. The way we handle controversy, conflict, and turbulence will determine the future of our institutions. An accentuation of suspicion, distrust, disruption, coercion, and violence will threaten, perhaps even destroy, intellectual freedom in the university.

The only hope of escaping this fate, we are told, is to return to the rule of reason as a means of resolving controversies, agreeing on purposes, and criticizing and affirming values:

> Appeals to common commitment by reason and persuasion, the pressure of opinion, the judgment of colleagues—these are the informal sanctions which cement the academic community and which administrators and governing boards, no less than professors, have a professional obligation to recognize as the principal modes of accommodation appropriate for a university community of scholars.[25]

But is reason—hard, impersonal, inflexible—the cement that will hold us together? Will reason release the spirit as well as discipline the mind of man? Writing about the traditional view that cognition is the only dependable way of knowing, two Berkeley political scientists said recently:

> The only legitimate instrument of knowledge is systematic cognition, and the only acceptable mode of discourse is the cognitive mode. Other paths to knowledge are suspect. Everything tainted with the personal, the subjective, and the passionate is suppressed, or dismissed as prejudice or path-

ology. A bureaucrat who based his decisions upon, say, intuition, dialectical reason, empathic awareness, or even common sense, would be guilty of misconduct.[26]

Reason is capable of reducing human experience and human values to juiceless formality, lifeless logic, unfeeling abstraction. What can be done to restore human significance to learning? It would help, at least, if we were to rescue literature from the putterings of the grammarians, save music from the musicologists, liberate art from the historians, cultivate the sensibilities as well as the higher mental processes, take liberal education away from the specialists who can be nothing else, and see man whole in an environment of enormous complexity.

Only teachers whose learning has embraced these qualities are capable of joining students in a search for the meaning of life, the means of human renewal, and the methods of coupling individuality with a deep commitment to the social welfare. Unfortunately, such teachers are scarce, not only in the great universities, but also in many small colleges.

If scholars were humble, they could join students in searching for the qualities and experiences which make men free, which exalt their humanity, and save them from dehumanization by a society characterized by large-scale organization. If all the members of the university were to join in this quest, they could restore the sense of community and commitment to institutions now torn with dissension and bereft of common purposes and values.

[1]Clark Kerr. *New Challenges to the College and University*. Berkeley, Calif.: Carnegie Commission on Higher Education, 1969, pp. 264-265.

[2]J.K. Galbraith. *The New Industrial State*. Boston: Houghton Mifflin, 1967, p. 291.

[3]Arthur R. Jensen. "How Much Can We Boost IQ and Scholastic Achievement?" *Harvard Educational Review* 39:1, Winter, 1969, pp. 1-123.

[4]*Daily Californian*, April 23, 1969.

[5]"Joint Statement on Rights and Freedoms of Students," *AAUP Bulletin* 54:258-261, Summer, 1968.

[6]Charles Frankel, "Rights and Responsibilities in the Student-College Relationship," pp. 232-251 in L.E. Dennis and J.F. Kauffman (editors), *The College and the Student*. Washington, D.C.: American Council on Education, 1966.

[7]R.M. MacIver. *Academic Freedom in Our Time*. New York: Columbia University Press, 1955, p. 206.

[8]*Ibid.*, p. 224.

[9]Sidney Hook. *Education for Modern Man*. New York: The Dial Press, 1946, p. 72.

[10]R.C. Wilson and J.G. Gaff. "Student Voice—Faculty Response." Berkeley, Calif.: Center for Research and Development in Higher Education, Preliminary draft of a report.

[11]Sir Douglas Logan. *Report by the Principal on the Work of the University During the Year 1968-69*. London: University of London, 1969, p. 7.

[12]J.W. Garbarino, "Professional Negotiations in Education," *Industrial Relations* 7:93-106, February, 1968.

[13]Clark Kerr. *New Challenges to the College and University*. Berkeley, Calif.: Carnegie Commission on Higher Education, 1969.

[14]Michael Beloff. *The Plateglass Universities*. London: Secker and Warbur, 1968, p. 188.

[15]William Deegan, T.R. McConnell, Kenneth Mortimer, and Harriet Stull, *Joint Participation in Decision Making: A Study of Faculty Government and Faculty-Administrative Consultation at Fresno State College*. Berkeley: Center for Research and Development in Higher Education, University of California, May, 1969.

[16]J.C. Livingston, "The Academic Senate Under Fire," paper presented at the 24th National Conference on Higher Education. Chicago: March 4, 1969, mimeographed.

[17]Clark Byse, "Collective Bargaining and Unionism in American Higher Education: Some Preliminary Comments," address delivered at the Danforth Foundation Workshop on Liberal Arts Education. Colorado Springs, Colo.: mimeographed.

[18]Israel Kugler. *AAUP and AFT—Which Way for the Professors?* (Reprinted and revised from *Changing Education*.) Washington, D.C.: American Federation of Teachers.

[19]*Ibid.*

[20]S.H. Kadish, "The Strike and the Professoriat," *AAUP Bulletin*, Vol. 45, pp. 160-168, June, 1968.

[21]"Statement on Faculty Participation in Strikes", *AAUP Bulletin*, Vol. 45: p. 157, June 1968.

[22]S.H. Kadish, *op. cit.*

[23] J.W. Garbarino, *op. cit.*

[24]*Chronicle of Higher Education*, October 28, 1968.

[25]S.H. Kadish, *op. cit.*

[26] Sheldon Wolin and John Schaar, "Berkeley: The Battle of People's Park," *The New York Review of Books*, June, 1969.

Precis

There is nothing useful or pat that can be said about all students. Although unjust percentages of college students are the children of the white and the rich, students as a group are probably more representative of the society's classes, ethnic groups, and quirks of opinion than any professional group or community in the country. Thus there can validly be wide debate about student opinion.

No matter how you slice the samples, though, it is obvious that students are in revolt. The relevant question is not why students are in revolt; the question is why are they the first to revolt. The answer is that they are brighter than most people, have less emotion invested in lies, and have more time than most to think about the direction of society.

To answer the question underlying this seminar, I will tell you what students want. It was expressed by a simple demand shouted at Army troops at the Pentagon and at National Guardsmen in Berkeley: "Join us!"

But what is meant by the demand "Join us!"? What's the program, who's the directorate, where's it going? To use a cliche of movement politics, our program rests on our analysis. The analysis is roughly as follows: American universities are integral parts—intellectual service stations—of a social order that is vicious, racist, warlike, authoritarian, immoral, and incompetent.

"Join us!" means building a new society in the hollow shell of the old, and building a new university in the shell of the outdated institutions we now have. It means transforming schools into something totally different from what they look like today. Schools would be free places where anyone, at any age, could go when he wanted to learn something, when he wanted to talk about ideas with other people, when he wanted to find a book about anything at all.

To make a life for themselves that is sane and human, valuing life and being able to trust their neighbors, a life during which they can tell their children they did something to better, instead of worsen, the human condition for at least a handful of people—that is what my generation wants to do.

STUDENT INTERESTS IN
VALUE CHANGE AND POWER CONFLICT

Susan S. Lloyd-Jones
Past Editor
College Press Service

You have asked me here to speak about value change. It is clear that this seminar, like any number of other meetings of intelligent and good liberal administrators, is a social ritual like the cocktail party, a commission of inquiry, or a war. The rules are well known; the social and political gavottes are plotted by tradition.

I am here as the token student, and no matter what I say you are prepared to say that it is idealistic, intelligent, worth consideration, and a little ahead of its time. In passing, you hope, you will learn something about "what students want," which means you think of yourselves as collective bargaining agents and of me as, to use a term many of you will remember from democratic socialist days, a fink.

Student Opinion

Luckily, I can't fink. There is nothing useful or pat that can be said about all students. The French anarchist, Daniel Cohn-Bendit, put it well:

> There are six million of us, sometimes treated as mere children, sometimes as adults. We work, but produce nothing. Often we have no money, but few of us are really poor. Although most of us come from the middle class, we do not always behave like them. The girls among us look like boys

but are not sure whether they really want to be boys. We look upon our professors as part father, part boss and part teacher, and can't quite make up our minds about them.

Some of us are destined to control the nation, others will become poorly paid professional hacks—but every one of us is privileged for all that. We include followers of *The Guardian* and other militant journals, assiduous readers of *Time* magazine, and devotees of baseball and movies, hippies, crammers, spoilt rich kids who never graduate, girls who will marry during their first year, but meanwhile study law, languages and even psychology; dunces, duds, future mathematicians and doctors.

"How can one 'understand' modern students?" Cohn-Bendit goes on to ask, and answers, "only by understanding their place in society."

A popular myth is abroad that the place of students in society is on the fringe, in a state of limbo before becoming full-fledged consumers and workers; drug-ridden, mystically minded and besotted with calculus and Chaucer, far from the reality of everyday Americans. Thus, it is maintained, students, who grew up in security and comfort unknown to other Americans, are selfish and strange in their willingness to revolt, in their demand that the social order change.

Nothing could be further from the truth. Although unjust percentages of college students are the children of the white and the rich, students as a group are probably more representative of the society's classes, ethnic groups, and quirks of opinion than any professional group or community in the country. Thus there can validly be wide debate about student opinion.

A recent Louis Harris poll, released near the end of May, said a heavy majority of college students agreed with the "radical" idea that their schools are not only bad schools but also do evil things in support of war and racism. Not all of them are ready to burn down buildings, but certainly they are not content with things the way they are, and most of them sympathize with the efforts of activists. The poll, curiously enough, got little coverage in the national press the weekend it appeared; the commentators were too busy extolling a Gallup poll which came to the opposite conclusion—that most students were busy as little bees earning their degrees. When it comes to polls, as Nelson Rockefeller found out, you pays your money and you takes your choice.

Students in Revolt

No matter how you slice the samples, though, it is obvious that students are in revolt. Not all of them occupy buildings; some just grow their hair long, or leave the country, or refuse to work for business or the government. Numbers of building occupiers do not measure the scope of student discontent, as you know perhaps better than I. The relevant question is not why students are in revolt; the question is why are they the *first* to revolt. The answer is that they are brighter than most people, have less emotion invested in stupid lies, and have more time than most to think about the direction of society.

To answer the question underlying this seminar, I will tell you what students want. It was expressed by a simple demand shouted at Army troops at the Pentagon and at National Guardsmen in Berkeley. Join us! That it is not a demand subject to formalization, mediation, and arbitration will be taken by some of you as evidence that our generation is prey to irrationality, emotionalism, and inability to reason. The wiser will realize that the strangeness of the demand is a sign that not only are the things being demanded changing, but the format and arena of demands are also changing. Thus the title of this institute, with its implication that higher education is a static entity within which value change and power conflict can take place, is misleading.

The form, the method, and the legitimacy of so-called higher education is being challenged, not just by me but by students who wave flags as disparate as Wallaceite and Maoist, Young Americans for Freedom, and Students for a Democratic Society, technology freaks, and artsy-craftsies. All of these agree with a number of simple propositions that are flatly opposed to the current "educational" order.

All agree, most recently by a 13,000-2,000 majority here in Berkeley, that land is for people and the bayonets of the liberal status quo have no legitimacy.

All agree that the doctrines of equal justice under law and of individual participation through democracy are so much hot air. All agree that education which can turn out most of its graduates with nothing more than diplomas, a few friends, and a highly developed ability to take tests is a failure.

All agree that the property-sated, monoxide-choked *Americanus emptor* is a sad citizen for a would-be civilization. The liberal capitalism that counts the sale of cancer as a plus in its GNP is, by general agreement, not fit for human consumption.

It is, of course, not news to you that we don't like your social order. Not even very many of your generation like it. Last November, 40 percent of you voted with Hubert Humphrey to turn the country into a chrome-plated Sweden, 20 percent voted with Wallace to trade it in on South Africa, and your thin plurality decided they wanted nothing more than the same, only duller.

And so, during the last year, an assortment of students from SDS to YAF have engaged in a series of protests as varied as their characters. What is important about the takeovers and petitions and diploma refusals and turn-ins and walk-outs is that they are just the first use of symbolic or theatrical protest by Americans trying to paint their own versions of reality in an insane picture factory.

They will be joined by businessmen shredding their credit cards and growing their hair. They will be joined by small-town people deciding they won't send any more sons to Vietnam. They will even be joined by the traditionally apathetic working class whose real incomes, according to the President's Council of Economic Advisers, have risen by only 35 cents a month since 1965, the same four-year period during which corporate profits rose 40 percent.

An Analysis

But what is meant by the demand "Join us!"? What's the program, who's the directorate, where's it going? To use a cliche of movement politics (and politics of my generation are sometimes horribly cliche-ridden, perhaps the best evidence you could want

90

that we are listening to our college lectures), our program rests on our analysis.

The analysis, to be quick and dirty about it, is roughly as follows: American universities are integral parts—intellectual service stations—of a social order that is vicious, racist, war-like, authoritarian, immoral, and incompetent. America today is the highest development of some of the human race's most serious mistakes: the attempt to conquer, or at least severely maim, nature; the desire to control and exploit, rather than understand, man's nature; that queer creation of the Renaissance, the secular national state; the development of killing for sport; the submission of the social information system to commercial whims.

All of these were interesting experiments, but it is clear that they were losers. America, the state that tried them out, is the dinosaur of societies, and the troubles you read about in the newspapers are its death throes. The university is an integral part of that social order, and it is as doomed, to maintain the paleological metaphor, as the dinosaur's kidneys.

This society is being killed off by the people of Vietnam, who have plans for their country plainly superior to any thought up by the economic geniuses of AID, the Peace Corps, Litton Industries, or Michigan State University.

The society is being killed off by its lower classes and subcultures who are making demands it is not prepared or equipped to satisfy. And it is being killed off by the refusal of a whole generation to pay even lip service to its ideals, a generation which discovered they can't buy happiness, friends or life, and are dropping out of the Great American Buying Spree, the haircut and the death-wish.

"Join Us!"

What does "Join us!" mean? A philosophy professor from Massachusetts Institute of Technology, Huston Smith, writing in the *Wall Street Journal*, put it well:

How should we faculty, and administrators, and trustees

91

respond to the new currents on campus and the new student styles? Lists of ameliorative reforms only finesse the issue. For the basic issue in higher education today has become: On which side do the universities stand, the side of revolution or of reform-within-the-system? Do we believe that our capitalistic democracy can secure freedom and justice for all, or must there be a serious rearrangement in the bases of wealth, power and prestige?

If reform will do the job we should try to keep the university substantially as it is, doing so either baldly—by squashing the activists—or diplomatically by diverting their energies into ameliorative reforms—putting them on committees.

If revolution is indicated, we must work with them in ways that, being unprecedented, are less clear and are certain to require all the wisdom we can summon. Whatever our decision, we should not mistake the issue. It is not educationally procedural; it is socially substantive. Our students are forcing us to face the fundamental issue of how we can get the America we want.

"Join us!" means more than opposing the war in Vietnam. It means giving up the weird intellectual one-upmanship that, like the Kennedy-era fad for counter-insurgency and other hip liberal phrases, starts America's imperial wars in the first place.

"Join us!" means more than thinking about the current crop of progressive gestures—guaranteed income, token blacks in every college and federal subsidy to do-good groups. It means doing serious thinking about new kinds of governments and communities, new kinds of work and new ways of living day-to-day.

"Join us!" suggests by implication that the middle-aged and old in America are in some important way "against" the young majority, and it seems that this is so. It would hardly be too strong to say that the old in our culture hate and fear the young.

For what else can explain their peculiar obsession with police and guns and war? When a campus guard at Wittenberg University in Ohio shoots a 20-year-old student to death for visiting his girl friend in a dormitory, and is neither charged as a criminal nor hospitalized as a sick man, that tells us something about the structures and values we are living with. While America emulates and worships youth in its advertising, it reserves almost all power, economic and political, for the old.

America is not like other places: it is not usual for four or five percent of a country's adult males to be in uniform with guns, as police or soldiers. It can only happen in a queer place where somebody wants somebody else to be shot by a man in uniform.

America is not like other cultures: outside the Arab world it is not usual for large percentages of the population to be stoned on drugs all the time—on alcohol, the nerve relaxer; on nicotine the heart-speeder; and librium and stellazine and miltown and all the rest that are needed to keep the "adult" American character going in this supposedly "civilized" American culture.

Harvard physicist George Wald calls all these things indicators of American preoccupation with death and so-called "death-wish" activities. It follows that young people, fighting against that death-wish (from the destruction of the Grand Canyon to the building of nuclear weapons) are fighting in the name of life—life they see being bartered and compromised every day by statesmen and their overkill.

To say "Join us!" is to echo the old cry of the First International: Power to the People. In modern America that phrase has become virtually meaningless, used as it is by all the politicians trying to pretend that a vote means something, that decisions about the lives of everyone in this country are not made by the few men with the economic power to influence the course of military and political events. Students who worked in New Hampshire, in California, in Oregon, and in Chicago in 1968 found out how far America's political structure really is from the people. It must be brought back.

Joining means using the technology for what it's worth. One reason many students consider their time in college wasted is that they spend so much of it learning series of facts and figures and places and names and dates, and reeling them off at term's end on an exam. They know that machines probably used right now by professors doing Defense Department research could be giving them instant access to facts and figures they need to solve a problem or formulate a proposal in some area. When they read about planners and architects in Texas drawing up schemes of towns organized with information systems paralleling electricity and water systems (next to the phone booth a plug-in to the data bank where a passer-by can get information or documents he wants flashed on a television screen). Students can feel pretty silly reciting the dates of major American wars in a classroom.

Joining means thinking of ourselves as living in a constituency of six billion people, a whole planet's worth, rather than one of 200 million Americans. It means abandoning the futile and destructive chauvinism, condescension, and greed with which Americans have historically looked out on the world.

A New University

"Join us!" means building a new society in the hollow shell of the old, and building a new university in the shell of the outdated institutions we now have. That doesn't mean reforming them— putting more students on faculty committees, starting more jazzy-sounding courses, hiring a couple more black professors. It means transforming schools into something totally different from what they look like today.

Colleges would be places where people go to learn things that will be useful to them in their lives, or things they want to know just for the hell of it, and places where anybody could go for that purpose. They would not be places where the manpower needs of business and government are filled, or where the children of the rich are sent to be baby-sat for four years.

As Cohn-Bendit said, "In a truly democratic society, everyone would have a chance to be educated; there would be no student class as such." Schools would be free places where anyone, at any age, could go when he wanted to learn something, when he wanted to talk about ideas with other people, when he wanted to find a book about anything at all. The black students who last year "made it" to the white universities, only to discover that the schools had nothing for them, taught all of us to ask the most important question about our colleges: Who are they for?

94

Failure of Reason

A lot has been said in recent months about reason—the god of modern education and the hope of mankind. The universities have been collapsing, say the liberals, because students have lost faith in reason as the ultimate arbiter of human affairs.

To those of my generation who stand back and try to give the American world a good look, reason is a meaningless arrangement of six letters. It seems to us that if the system were founded and based on reason, as we are told, it would follow that its institutions would be flexible and responsive, that the application of reason to their activities would make a difference. If only the right arguments could be marshalled, or the right people set down to listen to them, the war in Vietnam would be ended, marijuana would be legalized, the ABM would be scrapped, and ghettoes would be a thing of the past.

It has become more and more clear that the strange, convoluted and rather quaint "reason" our good liberal elders appeal to is something with rather limited powers. It can call club- and chemical-wielding cops against unarmed students, but it cannot run a simple cost-benefit check on a missile. It can limit black enrollment at a college with exquisite mathematical grace, but it cannot calculate a strategy against poverty. It can build bomber bases around the world, but it can't design a liveable college dormitory.

The point isn't lost on the young; what America calls reasonable seems to them often more than a little insane.

They listen to the Army lying itself into a corner for more than a year about the slaughter with chemical-biological weapons of 6,400 sheep in Utah, and they watch every public official in Utah cover up because they'd rather keep a lucrative military installation in their state than refuse to take a chance with human life.

They see nine policemen in Orangeburg, S.C., walk out of court free after opening fire on a group of black students, killing three, and injuring scores of others in a clear case of police aggression.

They find out, when a group of Canadian students try it, that taking axes to a computer will get you a ten-year prison sentence; while accidentally killing a college student, if you're a campus guard who spots him visiting his girl friend, is quite all right.

They hear a United States senator tell his colleagues that "If we have to start over with another Adam and Eve, I want them to be Americans, and I want them here and not in Europe."

And they are told every day that using Ultra Brite toothpaste and buying a new pair of bellbottoms will make them happier and smarter and improve their sex life.

Why Students Rebel

Most students are not compelled by some great ideological cause. They begin to rebel because they have been cornered by a system that won't let them live in ways they think are sane and human.

They may not want to kill Vietnamese, but they find that feeling illegal at their local draft boards. They may not want to work in business or the government or universities, but they find themselves pressured by families and schools who think those the only means to success. They may not believe in marriage as an institution, but they find that when they try to live as a couple without that license they are discriminated against in every quarter.

They might want to live in communes, but they find themselves harassed by police and neighbors who can't understand why anyone would live that way. They may try to work with the poor or the blacks, and come smack up against the society's defenses against granting power to the minorities, the disaffected, and the poor.

To make a life for themselves that is sane and human, valuing life and being able to trust their neighbors, a life that will let them be at peace with their consciences and with all other men, a life during which they can tell their children they did something to better, instead of worsen, the human condition for at least a

96

handful of people—that is what my generation wants to do.

Join us!

Precis

The current crisis of the university, as that of the wider society, is a crisis of legitimacy. Not only are the decision-making processes within the university being called into question today, but also the university as it has functioned traditionally in society is being challenged.

The impetus for this challenge to the system of higher education in America, just as the impetus for revolutionary change in the national order, is coming from the black minority. It is, therefore, absolutely vital to the preservation of higher education that the black student movement be analyzed, discussed, and understood.

Three concepts embraced by nearly all black student groups today are self-pride, self-defense, and self-determination. It is this last concept which inevitably leads to conflict between black students and the university. To be master of one's own destiny requires power. Thus, the basic issue of contention in the university for minority students is the acquisition, distribution, and use of power.

Two important facts should be noted. First, the most prevalent tactics used by black students to gain concessions from the university are non-violent and moderate. Second, the goals of the black student movement are positive and constructive. For blacks, the university, if it can be transformed, offers hope of becoming a most effective tool in the task of rebuilding black America.

Black studies is undoubtedly the best known of all black student programs. Almost every accredited university with a minority student enrollment either has some type of black studies or ethnic studies program or is in the process of developing one. The fact that blacks have been able to produce changes in the institution to make it more responsive to the needs of blacks has created a chain reaction. Many white students have begun to protest the education they are receiving.

To date, most campus conflicts have been between students and administrators. The real conflict will erupt when faculties begin to resist the growth of student power. The faculty has a vested interest in maintaining the present system with few modifications. Black students have no vested interests in the present university structure. Therefore, it can be expected that blacks will continue seeking to obtain power and control over their destinies within the university.

MINORITY INTERESTS IN VALUE CHANGE AND POWER CONFLICT

Virgil Roberts
Graduate Student
University of California, Los Angeles

Much has been written and said recently about us living in a period of revolutionary change. One has only to take a cursory glance at the social phenomena increasingly prevalent in the past few years to be convinced that the fabric of the American social order is beginning to come apart at the seams.

Crisis of Legitimacy

The traditional goals and values and the basic institutions of society are today continually questioned and criticized. Specifically, a crisis of legitimacy has evolved in the American leviathan. This crisis is manifested by the unwillingness of significant numbers of citizens to acquiesce to the decisions made by the authoritative decision-makers within the society.

The best example is, of course, the opposition to the war in Vietnam and the anti-draft movement. There are also other examples of the general breakdown in the legitimacy of the system that deserve some mention. The conservative attack upon the Supreme Court demonstrates the growing lack of support for that institution as an authoritative decision-making body.

The Civil Rights Movement is another important indicator of the growing opposition to the legitimacy of the system. The growing revolt of welfare recipients is yet another example of the profound questioning of the system that is taking place within the contemporary social context. There are numerous other recent developments that could be listed to support the hypothesis that a crisis in legitimacy is developing but only one other will be mentioned—the black student movement.

The student movement represents an important component of current history which merits serious analysis. However, before entering into a discussion of the student movement in general and the black student movement more specifically, it is first necessary to make a brief descriptive analysis of contemporary society. Looking at contemporary society will aid in explaining the genesis of the contemporary crisis of legitimacy. It will also provide a perspective for analyzing and viewing the contemporary black student movement.

Society in Transition

When viewed in a worldwide historical context, the growth of the American economy has been nothing short of phenomenal. The GNP of the United States is approaching one trillion dollars a year. The average white American of today lives in an age of prosperity and affluence never before paralleled in the history of man even by the most powerful kings and potentates of the past.

Yet, in spite of the affluence of this period of history, which would lead one to expect growing support to be manifested in the system, there is widespread disaffection from the system. A generation ago there were only a few alienated people—most notably the beatniks. Today, the list is almost innumerable, covering great segments of the American population. There are the hippies, the yippies, revolutionary student groups, the minutemen, the John Birch Society, and numerous black organizations, to suggest a few.

The explanation is that America is in a period of transition from one social order to another. It is moving from an industrial, increasingly urbanized society into a post-industrial, technetronic

100

one characterized by the growth of the megalopolis and increased feelings of alienation by man in his prefabricated environment.

To illustrate the transition that is taking place, it might be helpful to look at society through the eyes of a person who supports the traditional norms and values of the culture—a cultural conservative. Such a person is watching all of the values he holds dear being transformed before his very eyes. First, he observes people all around him engaging in norm-violating behavior to achieve ill-defined goals of dubious value. He may sympathize with the goals or demands but is unable to comprehend the resort to illegal or unconventional strategies to achieve their implementation. And in no circumstance can he justify the use of violence to realize any end. Yet violence is openly being advocated as a tactic by many present day leaders.

There are other signs of the disintegration of social norms and values which can be observed by our cultural conservative. If he decides to relax from the fear-inducing world of deviant behavior by curling up with a good novel or reading a little poetry, he will find the literature saturated with four-letter words and the poetry unmetered, unrhymed, and barely comprehensible. Then, being deeply distressed, our hypothetical man may go to a movie only to find that the movies are sadistic and increasingly indecent sexually. Finally, in desperation, the cultural conservative may go to church to pray to God to save this damned insane society only to find that, instead of the normal mass or church service to which he is accustomed, there is a folk mass or a church service conducted to the music of a jazz combo.

This type of illustration could be developed indefinitely. However, the point is that traditional values are no longer accepted unquestioningly. The question that arises is what is causing the unrest and change in society? To answer this question, it is necessary to understand the effect that a highly technological society has had upon man.

The Technological Society

There are fundamentally two principles underlying the technological society.[1] First, if it is technologically possible to do something, then it must be done. This principle becomes central to the society and gradually supplants other values. Technological development becomes the foundation of ethics. As a result, America has spent billions of dollars in the last decade to put a man on the moon because it is possible, while during the same span of time thousands of people have died of starvation. Or, as another example, America contemplates deploying a thin ABM system at a cost of billions of dollars because it is possible, even if it may be outdated and ineffective by the time it is deployed. Simultaneously, those same people continue to starve. In other words, the technological society is more concerned about operationalizing the most recent technological advance or scientific discovery than meeting human needs and eradicating unnecessary social evils.

The second basic principle underlying the technological society is its continuous quest for maximal efficiency and output. This is most damaging in terms of the human personality. In order to receive maximum, efficient output from a human, tasks must be reduced to such a simple level that no creativity and very little judgment is required for the person to function. Man is reduced to the level of an automaton or a living cog in a massive industrial machine. If the human cog does not produce as programmed, it is crushed by the power of the machine-like system. The result is the creation of mass conformity and the gradual disappearance of individuality. The white collar worker of today is characterized by his identification with the firm or corporation. The goals of the corporation become the goals of the individual.

Concommitant with the assault launched by the technological society upon the individual's dignity and worth is the reduction of the individual to a super consumer whose only aim is to have more and to use more. If there is to be maximum output in society, there must be a market. That market is developed by creating an economy based upon waste and by convincing members of society to consume goods they often don't need. Thus, the individual is condemned to a humanoid existence by a system which he unknowingly perpetuates.

At any rate, there are two important ramifications of the technological society that have produced conflict. First, there is the centralization of power that is required for a society to advance rapidly. It is not coincidence that the growth in power and size of the national government closely parallels the growth in power and size of businesses and corporations.

The second consequence of the technological society is the increased feeling of alienation throughout the populace. People no longer feel as though they have any control over their lives or their government. Government seems so large and powerful and the individual, by comparison, is minuscule and impotent. More importantly, the future, which will bring with it a post-industrial, technetronic, cybernated age creating the possibility for new kinds of economic, political, and social organization, promises to merely perpetuate the alienation and powerlessness prevalent in the existing social order. Conflict arises when people make attempts to effect change in the social order to recover some control over their lives.

To make significant changes in the existing system, it is first necessary to acquire power. A democratization or redistribution of power must take place if meaningful social change is to be initiated. It took a decade, but black people eventually learned that the only way to deal with this society was by acquiring power. Appeals to conscience and moral suasion were not enough to cause change.

Lessons of the Civil Rights Movement

It is important to note that the Civil Rights Movement was the beginning of a snowballing challenge to the legitimacy of the present system. Beginning with Mrs. Rosa Parks in 1955, people began to stand up and reject the system. The Civil Rights Movement popularized and refined the use of unconventional or norm violative strategies as a means for the powerless to obtain a power position vis-a-vis the power structure.

It is symbolic and significant that the death of the Civil Rights Movement led to the birth of the Black Power Movement. Even more significant is the fact that immediately following the 1963 March on Washington, generally considered the end of the Civil

Rights Movement, the first major disruption of a university occurred at Berkeley in 1964 with the Free Speech Movement.

The Civil Rights Movement is important for discussion because it illustrates a number of points concerning protest activity and social change that are duplicated in the university. First, because of the rampant racism of America, blacks are in a position where the increasingly dehumanizing nature of society is focused most severely upon them.

Second, because of their oppressed existence, blacks are more alienated from the system and less encapsulated by it. As a result, blacks are likely to give up on the system much more readily than whites. Blacks have learned through experience to be pessimistic about achieving change through the system. Thus it requires relatively few nontraumatic defeats before blacks will give up on the system entirely and resort to uncoventional means of producing desired change.

Third, since blacks have, by and large, been on the periphery of the system, they possess an uncanny perspective and a lack of vested interests that enable them to generate creative ideas for the fundamental reorganization of society.

Fourth, whites who reject the present system and seek basic societal changes usually find themselves embracing the same general goals as blacks and employing strategies developed by blacks to attain their goals.

The last point that can be learned from the Civil Rights Movement is that those changes in society which benefit blacks more often than not also benefit whites. If blacks ever achieve the power to determine their destinies in this society, then all Americans will have achieved a power to determine their destinies.

The Black Student Movement

This brings us to the topic at hand—minority student interest in value change and power conflicts in the university. The crisis confronting the American university can be understood in light of the crisis affecting the country in general. The crisis of the university is also a crisis of legitimacy. Not only are the decision-making processes within the university being called into question today, but also the university as it has functioned traditionally in society is being challenged. The impetus for this challenge to the system of higher education in America, just as the impetus for revolutionary change in the national order, is coming from the black minority. It is therefore absolutely vital to the preservation of higher education that the black student movement be analyzed, discussed, and understood.

The black students who are currently pressing for fundamental and radical change are to be found primarily on white college campuses. This fact can be explained by a number of reasons. First, there are more blacks on white college campuses than ever before.

Second, the rise of black consciousness in this decade has had many important ramifications. Young black students have begun to gain pride in themselves, their culture, and their heritage. The growth of black consciousness has had the effect of amplifying the racist nature of the university. The cultural bias in textbooks, instructors, and research is becoming increasingly evident to black students.

Moreover, young blacks are becoming ever more critical of an education that does not equip them to cope with the problems confronting their communities or the problems of living in a post-industrial society. In addition, because of its emphasis on the brotherhood of all blacks, the growth of black consciousness has facilitated the birth of black student organizations.

A third explanation is that the white universities have attracted many of the top black students in the country. Consequently, in many instances, a white university contains a number of "super spooks" or young black intellectual giants. These youngsters are socially aware and race conscious students who are dedicated to using their innate abilities in attempting to devise a format for social change rather than engaging in reasoned discourse. Like most intellectuals of today, white and black, they are activist oriented.[2]

A fourth reason for the growth of protest activity on white

university and college campuses is the fact that many black students feel they must justify their participation in the system by aggressively seeking to foment change. The system is often viewed to be so corrupt that only those who are working for its total transformation can be said to be engaging in activity which is "relevant" or which relates to the needs of the black masses. As a consequence, black students attempt to justify their presence at a white university by pushing for a black studies program or the admission of more minority students and the hiring of black faculty.

Black Power

Finally, the advent of the Black Power Movement has had the effect of popularizing certain concepts. If the various nuances of black nationalism and black power that are manifested across the country are examined, three key concepts can be extracted. These concepts are embraced by nearly all black student groups. They are self-pride, self-defense, and self-determination. It is this last concept which inevitably leads to conflict between black students and the university. To be master of one's own destiny requires power. In the university context, it requires the acquisition of power that heretofore has never been exercised by students. This, then, is the basic issue of contention in the university for the minority student—the acquisition, distribution, and use of power.

Power has been defined in many different ways by many different men. However, I think most black students would accept the definition of power given by Huey P. Newton. Huey describes power as the ability to define phenomena and to make them act in a desired manner. Black students of today, for the most part, are serious and sincere about leading their people in a movement with designs of changing the social order. The students have enough sophistication to realize their goals can be accomplished only if they achieve a modicum of power.

The Civil Rights Movement taught that the only power the powerless possess is the power to disrupt the operation of the system. The fact that, in most instances, disrupting the system is against the law or is norm violative behavior is unimportant to students who maintain that the present system is illegitimate and

106

decadent. However, two important facts should be noted. First, the most prevalent tactics used by black students to gain concessions from the university are nonviolent and moderate. A good example is the recent seizure of the student union building by the black students of Cornell. The press emphasized the fact that the students had guns. But the fact that it was a nonviolent demonstration seems to have gone unnoticed.

The second point which should be emphasized is that the goals of the black student movement are positive and constructive. Black students are not making demands merely to bring the university tumbling down as is often the case with white radicals. For blacks, the university, if it can be transformed, offers hope of becoming a most effective tool in the task of rebuilding Black America. Therefore, the black student movement seeks to radically alter the function and purpose of the American University, not to destroy it.

The Malaise of the University

Before discussing the specific goals of the black student movement, it is important to understand the nature of the malaise currently gripping the university. The university in the post World War II period has increasingly absorbed the characteristics of the society about it. As a result, the same forces described earlier as being at play in the technological society run rampant in the university.

Universities operate on the same principles of maximal output and efficiency that society in general operates on. The resulting feelings of alienation and personal inadequacy are just as great if not greater within the university as in society in general. Students become IBM numbers and the professor a TV image. There is nothing inherently wrong with efficiency. However, efficiency should be considered in relation to the whole scheme of things. The alienation and disaffection that is caused by "time-saving" devices such as reducing the student to an IBM number challenges the propriety and efficacy of operating an institution on the basis of an economic principle.

The modern university unfortunately functions as a training

107

center for technocrats and functionaries of society. It should function as an educational center preparing man for living in a cybernated environment. What exists, in effect, is an institution which no longer emphasizes man and the inquiry into the experiences of man. The university has become a personnel department for the technological society. This fact is illustrated not only by the diminished value placed upon the individual in the university but also by the reward system for faculty within the university.

Faculty persons have two basic functions to fulfill in the higher education system. One is to do research; the other is to teach. The reward system of the university is such that only research is rewarded and honored. A university achieves stature and acclaim, not for its teachers but for its researchers. It receives governmental and private funds, not for its instructional program but for the quality of its investigative personnel.

Finally, promotions, salary raises, and other positive rewards are given, not to the man in the classroom but to the man in the library or the laboratory.

As if all this were not enough, there are positive and negative inducements in the types of rewards given. For example, it is considerably more profitable and prestigious to do research in nuclear physics than it is to do research in Hungarian literature. Admittedly this may be an extreme example, but it serves to dramatize that those types of research which are most rewarded are those which contribute most to the technological advancement of the culture irrespective of its benefit or harm to human civilization.

The university is as racist as any institution in America. This fact is most blatantly manifested by the curriculum in most universities. Only under the onslaught of persistent pressure from black students has there been even a minimal recognition of the Afro-American experience by the university.

The racism of the university is a great deal more unacceptable and damaging than it would be in another institution. The educational system is a primary component in the socialization

108

process. The educational system inculcates the values, norms, and traditions of a society into its youngsters. When that system is racist, it only serves to entrench and perpetuate evils which must be eradicated. This returns us to the goals of the black student movement.

Goals of the Black Student Movement

Black students are seeking power. The question which immediately enters the mind of most people is: Power to do what? That is the question which will be addressed.

The program that emanates from the black student movement of today has its foundation in an emerging worldwide humanism. Essentially, the black student seeks to acquire power to build a more humanistic society. He seeks a society with a capacity to embrace all types of people, a society that can withstand the challenges of a post-industrial era, that will return to man the power to determine his own destiny. He seeks a society founded upon the principle of the subserviency of technology to man, a society in which man is elevated to the status that technology commands today.

To achieve these idealistic goals, the student must confront the power structure of society. America, however, is an extremely powerful society that historically has been able to coopt and dissipate many dissident movements. Consequently, to have any chance of success, America must be challenged in a weak, yet vital sector. The university is just such a sector. It is extremely important as an agency of socialization and as an authoritative allocator of values. It is also highly vulnerable. A university cannot function effectively or properly in an armed camp atmosphere. As pointed out earlier, the university is presently in a state of malaise and seeking to redefine itself in order to remain viable in a rapidly changing environment.

Black Studies

In light of the general goals of the black student movement and the environment in which the students operate, the programs generated by black students are understandable and calculable.

Black studies is undoubtedly the best known of all black student programs. The demand for a black studies program is usually accompanied by demands for an all-black faculty within the program, complete autonomy of the department or program within the university administrative structure, student participation in all decisions affecting the black studies program, and increased enrollment of minority students in the university even if it requires remedial programs to prepare them for college level material.

The original demands for black studies were met by staunch opposition. Today, almost every accredited university with a minority student enrollment either has some type of black studies or ethnic studies program or is in the process of developing one. More important than black studies per se is the effect it has had upon the university.

The fact that blacks have been able to produce changes in the institution to make it more responsive to the needs of blacks has created a chain reaction. Many white students have begun to protest the education they are receiving. Moreover, they are making the same type of demands that blacks have been making. They are seeking to become part of the decision-making processes of the university, and they are seeking an education which relates more readily to the rapidly changing society.

Upon closer analysis, one will notice a number of inherent assumptions in the black student demands for black studies that provide some insight into the movement. First, there is an assumption that today a college education is a right. There seems to be a perception on the part of young black students that education is a requisite for survival. A few black student groups have demanded that all black applicants for college be accepted. Black students see the purpose of the university as teaching and therefore feel that the university could adjust to teach any and all incoming students.

Second, black students are neohumanists and believe that the emphasis of education should be man and the experience of man.

Third, there is a liberal, middle-class bias for education as a tool of social change that is expressed by most black studies programs. The substantive portion of most black studies programs is based on the idea of developing a black intellectual cadre which will then be able to come to grips with the manifold problems of the "Dark Ghetto." In all black studies programs there is the idea of turning intellectual thought into social action. This is achieved by having different types of community action programs built into the curriculum.

Finally, it is generally assumed that black studies is a tactic to gain power within the university and not an end in itself. The black student movement is relatively new and is still in the process of developing goals and ideology. However, one thing is certain. If a group has power, then its options are open. Black students must keep their options open because they remain unsure as to ultimate goals. This is the reason that black students demand autonomy for their programs. If the need for change should arise, blacks want to be in a position to make such a change in their program without having to fight for it.

Campus Power Conflicts

If we look to the future, more strife and power conflicts appear due. To date, most conflicts have been between students and administrators. The real conflict will erupt when faculties begin to resist the growth of student power. The power relationship between faculty and students is an inverse ratio. The more voice the students have in decision-making, the less the voice of the faculty.

The faculty has a vested interest in the present system and therefore will seek to maintain it with only a few modifications. Black students have no vested interests in the present university structure. Therefore, it can be expected that blacks will be seeking to obtain power and control over their destinies within the university.

If the university can overcome the malaise that grips it and jump forward to the future to become an institution that has transcended the monumental problems of the present, it may provide a paradigm for social change. To make such a change there must be a redistribution of power in the university and eventually there must be a redistribution of power throughout society. This will not be accomplished without much conflict. For as a great man, Frederick Douglass, once said, "There can be no progress without struggle."

---

[1]For an extensive discussion of the effects of the technological society see Erich Fromm. *The Revolution of Hope*. Evanston, Ill.: Harper & Row, 1968.

[2]See Paul Jacobs and Saul Landau. *The New Radicals*. New York: Random House, 1966, for a discussion of the intellectual as a social type.

Precis

The society toward which we are moving will be a learning society. The university will occupy a central position in this new learning society because the most important form of power in the future will be knowledge.

The search for truth has always been the announced aim of learning at all times. However, the university's assurance that its concept of truth is adequate to the demands of the future learning society seems to have been shaken. The attack on this fundamental value has come primarily from forces within, rather than without, the university.

A growing number of faculty and students are arguing that study, evaluation of evidence, and recommendations for future studies by the university are no longer relevant to the demands of the moment. This group urges the university to involve itself in action programs designed to solve pressing social problems. This criticism has cast doubt on the importance of the university as a purely rational and critical institution. Perhaps the search for truth is no longer adequate to the demands being placed on the university by society.

What I believe is emerging from our turmoil is a growing conviction that the university's accepted concept of truth as its highest value must expand to include a commitment to social justice. Unless the university proves by its actions that it is concerned about justice, all its talk about truth may be mere rhetoric.

The university at the moment has no firm structure. The administrator's power is difficult to define. Nevertheless, the administrator has a special function to perform at a time of transition like the present. No one else can focus attention on the new structures which can help to embody for the university its new concern for truth and justice.

Administrators, faculty, and students need to work together to invent situations in which the two imperatives of the university can be realized at the policy-making level of the institution. If these joint efforts can succeed in enlarging the value system of the university in a visible way, they will have justified the expectation that the university should have a central position in the post-industrial society.

114

VALUE CHANGE AND POWER CONFLICT: THE ADMINISTRATIVE INTEREST

Rosemary Park
Vice-Chancellor for Student and Curricular Affairs
University of California, Los Angeles

The question implied by the title of this paper is an essentially modern one, at least when raised in the context of the university. It is also an immensely important one because of the nature of the society toward which we are moving. There is general agreement that this society will be a learning society, which means that the university will not only continue as a channel for upward social mobility, but also that it will become the agent for coping with the human obsolescence produced by the continuing productivity of our technology.

Knowledge: the Power of the Future

Daniel Bell, of Columbia University, and others have repeatedly assigned to the university a central position in this new learning society. Their judgment is based on the prediction that knowledge will be the form of power in the future. It will surpass the older forms of power—ownership of land, wealth, and the means of industrial production. As the producer of knowledge, or at least as its disseminator, the university in a genuine sense will determine the strength and the quality of the future.

What is happening at the heart of the university today may decide not only the kind of leadership which the younger generation can provide to the decades ahead but also the structure and the values of the society which this generation will attempt to lead. There could therefore be no more significant, no more complicated theme for consideration than that of value change and power conflict in the university today.

It is clear that something is going on now at the university which does not fit into the accepted concept of the institution. The title of this conference correctly assumes that essential matters like values are at stake. It is less clear what values, how necessary to the university's well-being, and who may be defending and who attacking them.

Significantly, the disturbance of the traditional university image is not confined to one nation or to one area. Unrest among university students is worldwide. This leads to the obvious conclusion that local problems must be merely incidental to a more widespread and profound malaise. An examination of the usual presuppositions of the university may help to identify this concern or imbalance which may indeed, as the conference implies, lie in a shift in values. It would not be difficult then to see a power conflict as the result of deeper changes within the university and amongst its basic assumptions.

The Search for Truth

However closely the university may have been associated with the values of its society in the past, the present century has encouraged the development of a less compliant and more critical attitude on the part of institutions of higher learning. Following the collapse of religious orthodoxy and associated with the burgeoning of scientific studies, the truth to which the university professed its highest devotion became identified with the results of the application of the so-called scientific method.

The search for truth has always been the announced aim of learning at all times. The method, however, by which the search was made has tended to determine the nature of the truth discovered. It is doubtful whether St. John the Evangelist meant what you and I may mean when we all assent to the hope, "Ye shall know the Truth and the Truth shall make you free." It may even be questioned whether we are totally in accord with Thomas

116

Jefferson when he spoke about self-evident truths and included among them that all men are created equal.

For us and for our university, truth is the result obtained by honest examination of facts and by constant testing of the conclusions as more information is discovered and higher levels of generalization are reached. The logic and rationality with which the facts are assembled and weighed are fundamental. It is essential also that all experiments and documents basic to attaining the facts and formulating the findings be replicable by and for others.

Around this process a community, the university, has evolved devoted to the pursuit of truth so defined. Both the procedures and the results have been readily shared here and abroad with all whose training enabled them to appreciate the significance of this activity. In this way the universities of the world have been linked by mutual interests across all sorts of national boundaries, and constitute a means of international exchange and understanding.

More important has been the fact that both at home and abroad the universities, through their scientific studies, have aided and abetted the development of a technology which has changed in quite revolutionary fashion the level of health and well-being in their societies. Whether in agriculture, in medicine, in industrial production, in military capability, or merely in the level of society's expectations of comfort, the university, through research and teaching, has wrought miracles. With such extraordinary accomplishments arising from a concern for the discovery of truth, it is understandable that the university should be envisaged as the source of hope for a new kind of society destined to emerge from our industrial age.

Although I believe that this description and its conclusion are correct, I must nevertheless confess, I can find little evidence that the university anticipates such a basic role or that it has any confidence that it can discharge such a central responsibility in the future. In some strange way the assurance that its concept of truth is adequate to the demands of the future seems to have been shaken.

As far as one can judge, the attack on this fundamental value has not been mounted primarily by forces outside the university, though there have always been many who questioned the inquiring spirit and critical mood of the university. The disaffection which one senses today comes from within the community of learners itself. On occasion it takes the form of almost total rejection of rational processes. More often, however, the use of language and disdain for evidence reflect the belief that the vaunted scientific method and its respect for facts may be useful in small areas but that other means of determining action need to be found.

Opposing Views

When one tries to analyze what these other means may be, it becomes evident that two different senses of time are involved. On the one hand are the majority of the faculty who have lived through one or two World Wars, who have seen the extraordinary technological developments proceeding from university work revolutionize custom and mores. For them change is not endemic but is related to the work of the university as presently conceived. Study, evaluation of evidence, and recommendation for future studies are the tasks of the university. The implementation of the recommendations is not a university responsibility, though individual faculty members may wish to involve themselves in practical programs as citizens but not as university professors.

On the other side and of contrary mind are a group who cannot reconcile themselves to the normal pace of academic innovation. Research and Development (R and D), however well financed or manned, are no longer relevant to the demands of the moment. Seeing the present injustices of society, the poverty, discrimination, and exploitation, this group feels deep outrage that the university has not long since directed its full energies to active eradication.

In many instances, their moral protest exceeds their consciousness of complexity. They say:

Time is running out. We cannot wait for analysis of the constituent parts of the problem. This is only a blind, a hypocritical device, to hide your unwillingness as an institution to assist in opening the privileged areas of our society to the exploited and disadvantaged.

Instead of increasing the energy applied to understanding the issues, this group urges the university to act and to lead society. They are convinced that, by involving itself in action, the university will find solutions which it cannot uncover in its usual rational fashion and at its normal pace. Because time is passing without action, they accuse their colleagues of insensitivity and cowardice.

These two groups within the university are opposed in their differing sense of urgency and in their justifications for action. The older group is inclined to take refuge in the importance of knowledge as the prerequisite for action. The other is skeptical of this scholarly integrity in the face of human misery. They prefer to urge empathetic experience and fervid, rather than reasoned, commitments to action programs. "At least we will have done something, while you are still studying the statistics."

These accents, of course, are reminiscent of other reversions to anti-intellectualism in our national life. In some contexts they even seem like an escape from the complexities of the problem into the simplistic solutions of the fascists of an earlier European generation.

Whatever may be their philosophical ancestry, the conscience and the guilt of large groups on the campus have responded actively and enthusiastically and in so doing have cast doubt on the importance of the university as a purely rational and critical institution. Perhaps the search for truth is not enough, either now or in that future presented by the learning society.

It may seem ironic that, under these conditions, members of the alienated group do not abandon the university and enlist the government or the church in their cause. On the contrary, they press to enter the university and to remain in it. If their criticism of the university's values were indeed a reversion to irrationality or a prelude to fascism, then the university would in all likelihood have been totally disregarded or would have been scheduled to be overwhelmed at a later date.

The fact that disruption centers in the university means, I believe, that the university is seen to be the solution and that both sides concede this fact. Change is required and expected by both groups. It is the speed of that change and its relation to knowledge which is in dispute. The discussion or confrontation will be held at the university and not elsewhere.

Commitment to Social Justice

It may be too early to foresee the result. What I believe is emerging from our turmoil is the growing conviction that the university's accepted concept of truth as its highest value must expand to include a commitment to social justice. Justice, said Disraeli, is truth in action. Such a modification of the university's values, or such an expansion, is not a radical alteration in its historical development. Social and personal ideals were scrutinized extensively by the theologians who manned the first American faculties. With the advent of the social sciences came the introduction of a more critical examination of social values. In the background, however, there was always the possibility, sometimes the conviction, that greater justice would result if all the facts could be studied and presented.

It is this last condition which is being questioned today. Is it indeed enough to study and present? Does the university not have a responsibility to sensitize and encourage its students to action in the cause of social justice? Should not its educational program demonstrate its own concern by, for instance, exerting all its capacities to provide education for disadvantaged minorities?

Unless the university proves by such actions that it is concerned about justice, all its talk about truth may be mere rhetoric too. Perhaps it is not that the younger group so much denigrates truth and rational process, though on occasion they appear to, as that they see the requirements of justice so much more clearly.

The task of the university is, then, to bring the pursuit of both justice and truth into conjunction as constituent parts of a new value system and to reveal to university students and to society its devotion to justice as vividly as it has manifested over the

120

centuries its concern for truth. How and in what manner can this enlargement of ultimate corporate concern be brought about? To respond will require some description of the university's internal structure.

The University's Internal Structure

Traditionally, the authority of the university has resided and been exercised through its hierarchical organization. This means that, from earliest time, some within the university knew more than others and were therefore masters. Some knew less and were either pupils, apprentices, or journeymen.

In the last century, the knowledge of which some had more and others less was acquired through the scientific method, whose product was the dynamic truth of science.

History will show, I believe, that this community devoted to the pursuit of truth and structured according to the degree of its mastery of knowledge began gradually to erode, at first in the sciences. It appears that the expansion of knowledge resulting from the scientific method was so extensive that it tended more and more to foster obsolescence among the older generation and at an increasingly alarming rate. Even Robert Oppenheimer is said to have remarked that he did not understand what young physicists were talking about.

Further inroads on the cohesion of the university's structure resulted from massive extramural funding for research whose nature and subject was determined solely by the chief faculty investigator. Possibly, too, the emergence of countless professional societies contributed to dissolving the campus unity by developing collegial relations across university borders between the experts in the increasingly narrow fields of specialization soon characteristic of all fields of learning.

It was more and more obvious, as the century progressed, that his standing in his discipline or in a subfield thereof, transcended for a faculty member his status or authority on his own campus. In the early stages of this development a faculty member established himself in his own field and then succeeded to a position of influence on his own campus. But this proved to be a strenuous kind of existence and, except for budget problems, most faculty members found less and less time to concern themselves with general campus matters. Lack of attendance at university faculty meetings was notorious, but the consequences were slight or, at any rate, did not have to be faced.

That consequences could be avoided was not because in some miraculous way a university could be run without a source of practical authority but rather because, into the vacuum created by faculty disinterest, was propelled, as it were by a law of nature, that most modern of university officials, the administrator. These officials owe their existence in the first place to the increasing size and complexity of modern educational institutions. The vast sums of money required to support university activities and the attendant accounting problems, the responsibilities for physical facilities, for health and safety, for feeding and policing, for public information and fund-raising as well as for educational programs and counseling, all these tasks and others of the modern university caused a bureaucracy to develop in the university comparable to that in any other large scale corporation.

At the head of the enterprise was a chief executive officer called president, or chancellor, who was entrusted with legal, financial, and educational responsibilities on behalf of the corporation by a governing board, variously called trustees, governors, corporators, fellows, or regents. Since this officer was normally the approved channel for all communication to the governing board from inside the institution, he possessed great practical authority.

In addition, this chief executive officer tended to acquire symbolic authority as well. By custom such officers were chosen more often than not from the ranks of university faculty, either in the home institution or outside. In this way faculty control of the institution seemed to be perpetuated. Although most faculty members realized that the president's ties to his original discipline had weakened, they nevertheless thought of him as one of themselves and considered that authority still rested with the faculty, no matter how vacated the seats at the faculty meeting might be.

122

This very abdication was a vote of confidence in the president's ability to identify with the hierarchical concept of university authority and its location among the older faculty. On their side, most presidents were properly respectful of ancient faculty prerogatives and defended the faculty and academic freedom against attacks launched from outside the university. Actually and symbolically, the administrator was in a position of considerable power. Not only did he control budgets but, by general agreement, he spoke for or interpreted the university to the public. However respectfully the faculty was referred to in ritual matters, its authority was rapidly becoming a rhetorical and not an actual entity at all.

Student Demands for Change

This modus operandi as between faculty and administrator has been recently legitimatized in an oblique and almost ironic fashion by the campus disturbances. The students and younger faculty, who were the pupils or at most the apprentices or journeymen of the old system, began to question the adequacy of the university's value system to cope with present problems and demand that the university exert itself in the furtherance of social justice. They directed their demands for change to the administrator, not to the faculty.

Apparently they did not doubt that the administrator could commit the whole institution to new ways of teaching and selecting students and to new forms of relationship with the community as well as to new allocations of funding for a variety of new activities, most of which would seek to enhance awareness on the part of the university of injustice in all its social forms. The student, by his demands, invested the administrator with the power to proclaim a new ethic and, by implication, a new distribution of authority in order to effect changes in accord with these new values.

As we all know, these student demands are stylized so that they appear to proceed out of the firm conviction that the student generation represents an irresistible force of history, whose function in Hegelian terminology is to oppose and even to destroy the existing structures in order to make possible greater justice and goodness in the future.

123

For the most part the faculty did not react in outrage at the attribution of almost total authority to the administrator which these disruptions revealed. They were grateful, I suppose, that someone else had to face the young enthusiasts and their self-righteousness. But before long it was clear that demands were being made by students and approved by administrators which questioned the ancient faculty prerogatives to say who shall be admitted and on what basis. Suddenly students appeared who were totally unqualified according to established standards and who were admitted at best to right historic injustice, at worst as a result of student and community intimidation.

At the same time, communities were requesting assistance in solving practical problems of urban redevelopment, police policy, and ghetto schools, but there were no ways in which to reward such faculty as might respond. There was grumbling about the quality of teaching. Instead of being characterized by respect and eagerness to learn the wisdom of the master, the classroom atmosphere had suddenly become cantankerous, supercilious, or sullen. In short, the community of learning founded on a hierarchy of learners has been dissolved, the old values are questioned, and the representatives of an honorable ethic are pushed aside from the seats of authority.

But it is not only in the classroom that the old community has disappeared. In the relation between the student and the university as a whole, a similar new mood has emerged. The alert faculty member had long since realized that he was teaching older students, more graduate students, more postdoctoral fellows. Perhaps he asked himself what this shift in age group might do to the old concepts of *alma mater* and of *in loco parentis*.

More probably he did not realize that something had changed until the student newspaper carried an account of a student discipline case in which the student was represented by one attorney and the university by another. What had happened to the kindly dean of students who suspended you for a prank and welcomed you back with no hard feelings next semester?

Apparently the concept that a student had a particular status in the community and was accountable first to the university and only secondarily to the civil authorities was disappearing. Just as the relationship between the faculty member and the university had changed, so had the position and responsibilities of the university toward the student.

A further complicating factor was the intrusion of community groups unasked into the consideration of what were formerly academic matters, e.g., the naming of heads of research institutes, the number of minority students to be admitted, etc. With these groups, too, the administrator was expected to cope.

Instead, then, of a community of learners organized by respect and consent which was removed from the outside community because it was thought to represent a devotion to truth beyond the ordinary citizen's and therefore received special status, there appeared to remain only a place, a group of people of different generations, and a sense of loss. I doubt that the administrator alone either could or would recreate the community which he has served or that he can proclaim some new value for it to embody, however much this may be expected by some students or countenanced by some presently baffled faculty.

New University Structures

If my analysis is right, the university at the moment has no firm structure, but there may be emerging a different set of priorities or values which can have clear effects upon what remains of an earlier structure.

This brings me to the second part of the original topic, power conflicts. Much of what we have experienced on the campus must appear like a contest for power over the university. There have been violence, intimidation, and demands enough. But as for the gaining of power by one side or the other, I can testify only to the disappearance of the old pyramidal structure. In spite of the student appeals to the chancellor, as the top of the structure, his power is still difficult to define. And I doubt that the chief executive officer has gained any more positive control than he ever had by the student action. Nevertheless, he has a special function to perform at a time of transition like the present. In the recent past at least half of the chief administrator's time was spent in what I call foreign affairs, for the most part off the campus. With an uncertain organizational pattern and a demand to enlarge the basic values of the university, the administrator will find his greatest and most pressing responsibilities at home.

No one else, I believe, can focus attention on the new structures which can help to embody for the university the new concern for truth and justice. What these will be in detail I am not sure. In attempting to define them, we shall be striving for what I shall call a participatory environment. I am not sure what I mean by participatory, but I know what I do not mean. I am not thinking of meetings of representatives of highly organized campus constituencies only interested in bargaining to win advantage for themselves. And yet I see this as a definite possibility.

In some institutions the faculty have occasionally resorted to trade union or similar adversary affiliations to advance their particular point of view. Should this testimony to the dissolution of the older community continue, there would soon be arrayed on the other side, not the governing board or the administrator, but the associated students with their legal counsel and their irreducible demands, for instance, that x percent of the English department's time be devoted to conferences, or to graduate teaching, or to committee assignments in the Student Union.

In such a depressing situation the administrative function would be to act primarily as custodian or keeper of the record of agreements finally achieved. That would be an easier job than the one I see for the president.

If the university dissolves into a series of adversary relationships, formulated by due process and legal counsel, it would become dependent, not on presidents, but on professional arbitrators, who would no doubt develop considerable expertise in university matters as they have in labor negotiations. Is this, however, a prospect for an institution which has moral obligations?

The Need to Work Together

The only escape from such a fate as becoming the prey of the

126

arbitrators is for the faculty, students, and administrators, realizing their relative impotence if they persist alone, to work to invent situations in which the two imperatives of the university can be realized at the policy-making level of the institution. University senates and policy commissions are important mechanisms.

More significant, I think, is the establishment in the departments of joint councils for the management of affairs which could unite the interests of both faculty and students, the one concerned for truth, the other especially for justice. In the mutual examination of matters in which both have interests, though quite different ones, it would become clear that the search for justice needs to become today as much a part of the university students' experience as the search for truth. Though Disraeli may have been simplifying the problem somewhat when he related them so closely, nevertheless the student needs scope in which to realize both imperatives or he will feel morally justified in destroying the university, which he sees as a bastion of hypocrisy.

Many new alignments will need to be developed within the university, some to the community, interpreted not only as government and industry but also as the disadvantaged and exploited. Others will arise out of the use made by faculty members of the student activities advisors who have worked for years with student organizations and know their aspirations and their capacities. This latter cooperation will improve the community experiences, which can become an integral part of many course offerings and which can serve as part of the university's response to the student need to find a more just community. Unless there is general concern among the faculty for the quality of these experiences, they may remain merely an unsophisticated outlet for "do-goodism" and not the intellectual challenge they should become.

Somewhere within this emerging structure, there will be need for an administrator who is not just an expediter but who can continually remind the whole constituency that the university is a moral as well as an intellectual institution. Perhaps not every chief administrator will possess this capacity. (There were after all only a handful of philosophers in Greece.) But I think it should be expected of him. For that reason most administrators should be young. They need to be able to identify with the demands of justice as well as of truth and especially they will need the fortitude to endure the endless participatory sessions which lie ahead. Out of these sessions can emerge a structure for the conduct of university affairs which may not re-establish the friendly sense of community of the past but which will better reflect the new values of the university.

If these joint efforts can succeed in enlarging the value system of the university in a visible way, they will have justified the expectation that the university should have a central position in the post-industrial society. It will no doubt be a learning society, but not just for those outside the university.

We are now progressing through an historic shift in university values which has been accompanied by disruption from one side and obtuseness on both sides. To realize the extraordinary possibilities ahead, those who have devoted themselves to the search for truth must expand their horizons. Those who pursue justice must remember that justice itself is blind, but the men who seek after her are not. The university's task today, as in the past, is to open ways to truth. But these paths must also help to lead to the more just society which the student demands of his future, today.